Collins Backroom Cooking Secrets

WALDMAN HOUSE PRESS
Minneapolis, Minnesota

*Dedicated to Kathy,
of course.*

Collins Backroom Cooking Secrets

Wild Game, Fish and Other Savories

by Tom Collins

Foreword by Ron Schara

Illustrations by Dennis Anderson

WALDMAN HOUSE PRESS

You may order single copies from the
publisher. Try your bookstore first.
Cover price plus $1.00 postage and handling.

Waldman House Press
519 North Third Street
Minneapolis, Minnesota 55401

Library of Congress Cataloging in Publication Data

Collins, Tom
    Collins Backroom cooking secrets.

    Includes index.
    1. Cookery (Game) 2. Cookery (Fish) I. Title.
II. Title: Backroom cooking secrets.
TX751.C64   641.6'91   80-21062
ISBN 0-931674-02-6

Printed in the United States of America
First Edition / Second Printing

CONTENTS

FOREWORD

Like tall oak trees and mighty rivers, the finer things in life often have small beginnings.

Keep that in mind if you ever venture into Minnesota's lake and pine North Country. On the shores of great Leech Lake, there's a small resort community named, "Walker." It's a one-street town mainly, a widespot in the woods lined with family-owned businesses to sustain the local folk (pop. 1,073) and keep the vacationing tourists satisfied.

Walker is easy to pass through because of its short Main Street. But most travelers don't and I wouldn't recommend it. For one thing, if you're looking for fishing tackle, bait buckets or a dozen nightcrawlers, Walker has more bait shops than drug stores. Fishing and hunting are the main reasons most folks live in Walker. Most visitors have the same objectives in mind.

That and to spend an evening of dining in Collins Cafe.

Collins Cafe is like a book with a plain cover and exciting contents. You'll find it, of course, on Walker's Main Street. From the front, Collins Cafe appears no different from the thousands of other cafes in thousands of other small towns in America.

The difference, however, shows up on the menu. On any given night, your menu choices may include Australian Rabbit as well as a New York Strip. The regular visitors to Walker are well aware of the unusual cuisine, of course. But I've often wondered how strangers react who are lucky enough to stumble into Collins Cafe unaware.

It must be like finding diamonds on a crabapple tree.

If so, Tom Collins planted the tree. It was for fun at first. Some wild game and wild fishes were gathered by friends and Tom Collins agreed to cook it.

But Tom Collins doesn't prepare food just to eat. His wild game dishes became celebrations. Nature never tasted so good.

One thing led to another and ... well, the word spread. That's how I first met Tom Collins. Somebody told me "I just had to go" to one of his wild game dinners.

I did and, well, you haven't lived until you taste a slice of elephant trunk in, of all places, Walker, Minnesota.

But I discovered more than exquisite dining. Tom Collins also is an avid sportsman who has long participated in the traditions of fishing and hunting — gathering your own food from the land. Most hunters and fishermen feel a sense of closeness to the earth for having shared its natural bounty.

Tom Collins adds this closeness to his wild game recipes. Which means you should like the taste of this book.

RON SCHARA
AWARD-WINNING COLUMNIST
FOR THE *Minneapolis Tribune*
AND AUTHOR OF RON SCHARA'S
MINNESOTA FISHING GUIDE

ABOUT THE AUTHOR

Although he was born in Lewiston, Idaho, Tom Collins spent much of his boyhood in Minnesota. It was in Minnesota's North Country where Collins first discovered the joys of eating fish from the pine-shrouded lakes and ruffed grouse from the aspen thickets. Being raised in a restaurant family, Collins eventually opened his own, "Collins Cafe" in Walker, Minnesota in 1963. Soon after, he began experimenting with wild game dinners for a "few of the boys." Today, Collins' fame as a wild game chef has spread far beyond the pine country of Minnesota. And the demand for his touch with fish and fowl is the reason for this book.

HERE'S HOW IT ALL BEGAN
FROM TOM COLLINS

Although I have hunted and fished for many years, I didn't "really get into" wild game until I bought my Restaurant in Walker, Minnesota.

Every fall a bunch of "us guys" — each getting hunting fever — would gather to discourse mightily about oncoming seasons and the ensuing hunt. Naturally the discussions eventually led to the ultimate destiny of all game — a dinner, of course.

Those early game dinners are just a fond memory now, but a memory no less. The festivities commenced at about noon of the assigned day. For the first few years, the dinners were strictly stag events.

Preparation of the game was an all day affair. So too was the preparation of the diners. Liquid refreshments flowed copiously as members of the group frequently visited the Restaurant to check on the progress of their favorite dish.

I recall one incident where a young fellow, glazed of eye and happy of countenance, greeted a visiting game warden and deposited a burlap bag on my kitchen floor. Sometime later when the bag was opened, I discoverd the contents to be a still-warm hind quarter of venison. Such were the trials and tribulations of a neophyte northwoods game cook.

We don't do this anymore. I no longer have ulcers either! This is not meant to be a confessional nor a directory of how to begin a game dinner. But I can't help but reminisce of the fine days when the fellowship was good and so was the game. The two seemed to work together.

Since those days, our annual blast has evolved from free-wheeling happy-go-lucky eat, drink and make merry affairs to somewhat more sophisticated and regrettably — to some of us — commercialized dinners.

X

Naturally, after several years of the same diet — moose, goose, duck, partridge, and a few fish — someone asked, "What do we do next year ?" Thus began the search for the exotics. It has been a lot of fun, and it has created a lot of interest.

I have found considerable interest and fascination from nearly everyone who has partaken of wild game. I have come to believe that wild game is held to be somewhat mysterious by many people, impossible to comprehend and extremely difficult to prepare. This is not true.

In my Restaurant (Collins Cafe) at Walker Minnesota, we have served wild game from all over the world. Elephant, hippopotamus, African lion, Dall sheep, llama, Rocky Mountain goat, and caribou have been served to many adventuresome people.

Over the years, two Vice Presidents, several Congressmen and Senators, a couple of Cabinet Members, a few Supreme Court Justices and a couple of English Lords have graced our humble tables. We also must not forget to mention a couple of University Presidents and assorted captains of industry.

As for how the "Back Room" got its name, it more or less evolved of its own volition. The room is located at the back end of the building and was used as a storage room. "Go to the back room" for one thing or another was heard several times a day.

We added some carpeting, paneling and table cloths, but the "Back Room" is still what it is called. So be it.

We have entertained the great and not so great over the years and reservations are a must for the "Back Room," being both a blessing and a curse. A blessing in that we appreciate the business that the room has engendered; a curse because the room is small and the knowledgeable faction (menu wise) won't settle for less, or even the same food in a different setting.

Maybe that is part of the mystique of the room as it certainly is not lavishly appointed. We like to think that the food has something to do with it. We serve a rather complete menu of gourmet foods from all over the world, but you guessed it, wild game is the most popular. Therefore, wild game is the reason for the "Back Room" and the "Back Room" is the reason for this book.

I sincerely hope you will use and enjoy the recipes written here and that they will give you dining pleasure.

Happy game cooking

Tom Collins

Tom Collins

WHAT'S NEEDED TO KNOW
FROM KATHY COLLINS BUXTON

"If you want to get involved in the restaurant business, you must start at the bottom and know every level," that's what my Dad told me as he showed me how to wash dishes in our family restaurant.

It was my introduction into the restaurant business.

Now almost twenty years later, I am teaching a Professional Chef Class, so things have progressed.

One must have a beginning and the recipes in this book will help you with your wild game. We have tried to make you feel comfortable with wild game meat. Some people lose control the first time they find a stringer of fish in their sink or a deer hanging in their garage or some "animal" in their refrigerator.

My first rule for cooking game meat is DON'T PANIC! Handled properly game meat can be delicious to your palate and served beautifully. A word of caution to the homemaker: Your attitude will determine how your family reacts. Positive thinking is the word. If you are excited to prepare it, your family will catch your enthusiasm. My two children consider venison their favorite meal. I serve many kinds of fowl, fish and game in my home and my family loves it. I also serve it to guests on many occasions and people are often surprised at how much they enjoyed the meal.

Our annual Wild Game dinners are the hit of the year at our Collins Restaurant in Walker, Minnesota. People fly in from all over the United States to participate. We have tri-state media coverage so we have proven that Wild Game can be something special. Don't be afraid to try these recipes. Most wild game should be treated like any domestic meat. We prepared a Wellington of Lion for a TV show and had a lot of doubters in the audience. But we served it on the air and everyone was surprised at how delicious it was. Of course you certainly don't have to get a lion to have a good meal.

My last words to you are, have fun! We have had many happy nights serving these recipes. It just takes someone to cook them and someone to enjoy eating good food. So enjoy, enjoy, enjoy!

Kathy Collins Buxton

Kathy Collins Buxton

WATERFOWL

WATERFOWL FIELD FACTS

Waterfowl require the following preparation and treatment: Immediate evisceration (gutting). Make an incision from the point of the breastbone to the vent and remove the entrails (intestines). Clean and wash the body cavity thoroughly, and cool quickly. Remove feathers as quickly as possible.

BREAST OF DUCK IN BRANDY SAUCE WITH WILD RICE

WHAT'S NEEDED:

1/4 pound butter
1/2 cup Cognac or Brandy
1/2 cup dry Sherry
2 Tablespoons grape jelly
4 duck breasts (8 fillets)
1 cup wild rice, rinsed well
2 cups water
1 teaspoon salt
arrowroot or cornstarch and water to form a thick paste

HERE'S HOW:

1. In a heavy fry pan, melt butter. Add Cognac, Sherry and jelly. Bring to a boil.
2. Add duck breasts. Cover, reduce to low heat. Simmer for 30 minutes or until tender.
3. Boil the rice in salted water, covered, until fluffy and tender.
4. Place duck breasts on hot wild rice. Thicken the sauce remaining in the pan with a mixture of arrowroot and water.
5. Pour sauce over duck and wild rice.

4 Servings

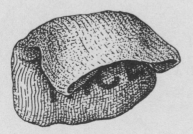

Fricassee of Duck

WHAT'S NEEDED:

>2 ducks, deboned, skinned, and cut into bite size pieces
>1/2 cup flour, seasoned with salt and pepper
>1/4 cup butter
>1 onion, minced
>2 bay leaves
>1 cup mushroom caps
>1 green pepper, sliced into thin rings
>1 cup water
>1/4 cup Burgundy wine

HERE'S HOW:

1. Dredge the duck pieces in the seasoned flour.
2. Put the butter, duck, onion, bay leaves, mushrooms and green pepper in a large skillet and brown the duck.
3. Add the water and wine, cover and simmer for 1 hour.

3-4 Servings

Glazed Duck
with Brandied Peach Sauce

WHAT'S NEEDED:

>1 whole duck per person
>salt and pepper
>Brandied Peach Sauce (see index)

HERE'S HOW:

1. Rub the inside of the duck with salt and pepper.
2. Bake in preheated 375 degree oven for approximately 1 hour. (This will give you a medium well duck, still a bit pink.) For a well done duck cook an additional 30 minutes.
3. Remove the duck from oven and brush with hot Brandied Peach Sauce. Brush repeatedly until a high glossy glaze is achieved.

Note:

Garnish with serrated orange halves or canned peach halves filled with red currant jelly.

DUCK STUFFED WITH ORANGES AND APPLES

WHAT'S NEEDED:

2 ducks
2 fresh oranges, peeled and cut into 1/2" cubes
2 fresh green apples, with peeling, cut into 1/2" cubes
juice of 1/2 lemon
6 strips of bacon
salt and coarse ground pepper

HERE'S HOW:

1. Season the ducks to taste with salt and pepper.
2. Combine the diced apple and orange, and stuff ducks with this mixture.
3. Place the ducks in a greased baking dish. Cover with the strips of bacon and bake (covered) at 350 degrees for 1 hour.
4. Remove the cover. Baste with lemon juice and return to 375 degree oven for 15-20 minutes.
5. Remove from oven and discard the stuffing and bacon.

2 Servings

DUCK STUFFED WITH SAUERKRAUT

WHAT'S NEEDED:

1 cup canned sauerkraut
2 Tablespoons brown sugar
1/8 cup diced onion
1/8 cup diced celery
salt and pepper
1 duck

HERE'S HOW:

1. Mix sauerkraut, brown sugar, onion and celery well. Salt and pepper to taste.
2. Place stuffing into cavity of duck and bake at 350 degrees for 1 hour and 15 minutes. (The duck should be slightly pink at this point.)
3. Cook approximately 30 minutes more at 350 degrees for well done duck. Stuffing may be discarded.

1 Serving

WILD DUCK WITH RICE

WHAT'S NEEDED:

2 wild ducks, skinned, deboned and cut into 1/2"
    chunks
1/4 cup butter
1 (16 ounce) can tomato sauce
4 ounces dry white wine
2 cloves garlic, minced very fine
1/2 onion, chopped fine
1 rib celery, diced fine
1 medium green pepper, diced medium
salt and pepper
dash cayenne pepper (optional)
1 cup regular white rice

HERE'S HOW:

1. Saute the duck in butter in a large fry pan.
2. Add the tomato sauce, wine, garlic, onion, celery and green pepper.
3. Season to taste with salt, pepper and cayenne.
4. Heat until boiling.
5. Add the rice, stir thoroughly.
6. Simmer over low heat, covered, until the rice is cooked — approximately 20 minutes.

Note:
Wild rice may be substituted for the white rice, however, it should be partially pre-cooked.

4 Servings

FRIED BREAST OF CANADA GOOSE WITH CHERRY SAUCE

WHAT'S NEEDED:

> 1 whole breast of goose, skinned and deboned (2 fillets)
> salt and pepper
> egg wash: 1 egg, 1 Tablespoon milk, mixed well
> 1/2 cup all purpose breading (seasoned coating mix)
> 3 Tablespoons butter
> Cherry Sauce (see index)

HERE'S HOW:

1. Season the meat with salt and pepper.
2. Dip in egg wash.
3. Dip in coating.
4. Fry in butter in a covered heavy fry pan on medium until tender, about 45 minutes.
5. Serve with Cherry Sauce.

4 Servings

ROAST CANADA HONKER WITH GINGER SAUCE

WHAT'S NEEDED:

> 1 (8-10 pound) oven-ready honker
> 4 Tablespoons butter, melted
> salt and pepper
> paprika
> Ginger Sauce (see index)

HERE'S HOW:

1. Place the goose in a baking pan.

2. Brush with butter and season with salt and pepper.
3. Dust with paprika.
4. Bake covered at 325 degrees for 1½ - 2 hours or until bird is tender. Uncover last 1/2 hour.
5. Remove bird from oven. Allow to cool slightly.
6. Slice the bird into portions for serving.
7. Serve with Ginger Sauce.

6-8 Servings

SAUTEED BREAST OF GOOSE

WHAT'S NEEDED:

1 cup flour
1/2 teaspoon salt
1/4 teaspoon pepper
2 whole deboned breasts of goose
1/4 cup butter
2 ounces dry Sherry
1/4 cup Sweet Sauce (see index)

HERE'S HOW:

1. Mix flour, salt and pepper together.
2. Slice goose breast thinly.
3. Dredge goose breasts in seasoned flour.
4. Brown in butter in hot skillet.
5. Reduce heat and add Sherry and Sweet Sauce.
6. Cover and simmer at low heat until tender.

4-6 Servings

BREAST OF CANADA GOOSE IN WHITE WINE SAUCE

WHAT'S NEEDED:

- 1/3 cup flour
- 1/2 teaspoon salt
- 1/4 teaspoon pepper
- 1 breast of goose, skinned and deboned (2 fillets)
- 1/4 cup butter
- 1/4 onion, diced very fine
- 1 pint Basic Cream Sauce (see index)
- 2 ounces dry white wine
- 1 ounce Brandy or Cognac

HERE'S HOW:

1. Mix the flour, salt and pepper together.
2. Dredge the goose fillets in the seasoned flour.
3. Saute the floured goose fillets in butter in heavy fry pan until golden brown.
4. Add the diced onion and saute until translucent.
5. Add the cream sauce, wine and Brandy.
6. Salt and pepper to taste.
7. Simmer covered for approximately 45 minutes to one hour.

4 Servings

UPLAND
GAME BIRDS

UPLAND GAME BIRDS

Partridge (ruffed grouse), sharptail, squab, quail and wild turkey are generally moist and tender if the classic gourmet approaches are adapted. Again I caution you, do NOT overcook them.

Don't blow your cool at the thought of Kievs, Cordon Bleus or Supremes. Use these birds interchangeably with any game bird recipe or with any of your favorite chicken recipes. To make them look even better, try garnishing with a canned peach half, dusted with cinnamon or nutmeg, or a canned pear half with a drop or two of Creme de Menthe. Fresh parsley, red or green grapes, orange or lemon slices or combinations of any of these mentioned will help to make your plate more appealing.

The partridge has often supplied camp meat for the deer hunting party. Here is a comfortable way to reduce this fine bird to something edible right at the campsite.

PARTRIDGE A LA WOODSMAN

WHAT'S NEEDED:

1 fresh partridge per person
1/2 cup cooking oil
salt and pepper
aluminum foil
1 roaring camp fire
26 ounces Yukon Jack (any good Bourbon or blend may be substituted)

HERE'S HOW:

1. Dress the bird. Skinning is permissible in woods.
2. If there is water handy, wash the bird.
3. Brush with cooking oil. Season with salt and pepper, wrap in foil and secure on long sharp stick.
4. Allow the roaring camp fire to be reduced to hot coals, usually taking 30-45 minutes. During this time one can prepare oneself mentally and spiritually for the magnificent repast by consuming half or any lesser portion of the Yukon Jack (or substitute spirits). You are now ready to cook the bird.
5. Expose the foil covered bird to the hot coals for 30-40 minutes.
6. Remove from foil and consume this delicacy with the remainder of the Yukon Jack.

PARTRIDGE IN BARBECUE SAUCE

WHAT'S NEEDED:

1 partridge per person
salt and pepper
paprika
butter
**Barbecue Sauce (see index) or your own concoction or
 any commercial brand that you like**

HERE'S HOW:

1. Split and disjoint the bird.
2. Season with salt and pepper and dust with paprika.
3. Saute in a heavy skillet in butter until brown.
4. Remove from heat and drain the butter from the pan.
5. Add Barbecue Sauce, enough to cover bird.
6. Simmer over low heat, covered for about 40 minutes or until tender.

1 Serving

Breast of Partridge Kiev

WHAT'S NEEDED:

1 deboned partridge breast
1/4 cup soft butter
1/2 clove garlic, minced to a pulp
1 teaspoon finely diced green onion
1/2 teaspoon chives
salt and pepper
1 egg white, beaten well
egg wash: 2 eggs, 2 Tablespoons milk, beaten together
1 cup all purpose breading (seasoned coating mix)

HERE'S HOW:

1. With a cleaver flatten partridge breast.
2. Blend the butter, garlic, onion and chives.
3. Stuff the partridge breast with this mixture.
4. Close the edges and press lightly to seal.
5. Refrigerate until butter mixture is solid.
6. Brush with egg white and freeze.
7. Remove from freezer, dip in egg wash then in breading.
8. Wrap in aluminum foil, return to freezer until needed.
9. Fry the Kiev in a deep fryer until browned, then place on a baking sheet and bake in 375 degree oven 45-60 minutes.

1 Serving

PARTRIDGE BAHAMAIAN

WHAT'S NEEDED:

> 2 whole deboned partridge breasts
> salt and pepper
> paprika
> 1/4 cup butter
> 1/8 teaspoon cumin
> juice of 1 fresh lime
> 2 cups water
> 2 chicken bouillon cubes

HERE'S HOW:

1. Season partridge with salt and pepper, dust with paprika.
2. Saute in melted butter, until golden brown. Add remaining ingredients.
3. Cover and reduce heat to low.
4. Simmer 45 minutes until tender.

Note:
This can be served on a bed of boiled white rice.

4 Servings

PARTRIDGE SWEET AND SOUR

WHAT'S NEEDED:

> 3 disjointed partridge
> 1/2 cup flour
> 3 Tablespoons cooking oil or butter
> 1 medium onion, diced fine
> 2 teaspoons English mustard

1/2 cup peach or apricot jam
1/2 cup canned tomato sauce
1/2 cup hot water and 2 beef bouillon cubes
3 teaspoons white cider vinegar
2 teaspoons soy sauce
1 teaspoon Worcestershire sauce

HERE'S HOW:

1. Dust the birds with flour and fry in oil or butter until brown. Remove birds.
2. Saute the onions in remaining oil or butter until they are translucent.
3. Add all other ingredients, including the browned partridge and simmer, covered, at low heat for about 30 minutes or until bird is tender.

3-4 Servings

BREAST OF PARTRIDGE CORDON BLEU

WHAT'S NEEDED:

1 deboned partridge breast (or any other upland game bird)

1 slice of thinly sliced smoked ham, per breast

1 slice of Swiss cheese, per breast

salt and pepper

1 egg white, beaten

egg wash: 1 egg, 1 Tablespoon milk, beaten together

1/2 cup all purpose breading (seasoned coating mix)

HERE'S HOW:

1. Flatten the breast with a cleaver. Place ham and cheese into each seasoned breast.
2. Flatten edges to seal ham and cheese mixture in breast.
3. Brush with egg white. Freeze.
4. Dip in egg wash. Coat with breading and refreeze. Repeat if necessary to form a good seal.
5. Fry in a deep fryer until golden brown, then bake 45-60 minutes in a 375 degree oven.

1-2 Servings

PARTRIDGE BAKED WITH SWEET-SOUR RASPBERRY GLAZE

WHAT'S NEEDED:

4 partridge
1/4 cup butter, melted
salt and pepper
1 package frozen raspberries
1/2 cup water
1/2 cup sugar
juice of 1/2 lemon
2 ounces blackberry Brandy or raspberry liqueur
arrowroot or cornstarch and water to form thick paste

HERE'S HOW:

1. Brush partridge with melted butter. Season with salt and pepper. Place in well greased baking dish.
2. Cover tightly. Bake in fairly hot oven at 375 degrees for 45-50 minutes.
3. Remove from oven. Brush with glaze.
4. Reduce heat to 300 degrees and return to oven for 5-10 minutes.
5. Repeat steps 3 and 4 until well glazed.

**HERE'S HOW
FOR GLAZE:**

1. Thaw raspberries.
2. Add water, sugar, lemon juice, Brandy or liqueur.
3. Heat to simmering and thicken slightly with arrowroot or cornstarch and water paste.

4 Servings

CACCIATORE OF GAME BIRDS

WHAT'S NEEDED:

3 game birds, cleaned and disjointed
1/2 cup flour seasoned to taste with salt and pepper
1/2 cup cooking oil
1 onion, chopped coarsely
1 green pepper, diced coarsely
2 cloves garlic, diced to a pulp
1/2 cup canned mushroom caps
1 (#2-1/2) can tomatoes, crushed, with juice
1 cup of Madeira wine
1/4 teaspoon crushed oregano
1/4 teaspoon sweet basil
1/4 teaspoon salt
1/8 teaspoon black pepper

HERE'S HOW:

1. Dip birds in seasoned flour.
2. Saute birds in hot cooking oil in a heavy pan until golden brown. Remove and place in a roast pan or baking dish.
3. Saute the onion, green pepper, garlic and mushrooms in a small pan with a little cooking oil until they are golden brown. Add the tomatoes with juice, wine and seasonings.
4. Mix well and pour over the game birds. Cover and bake at 350 degrees approximately 1 hour or until birds are tender.

4-6 Servings

20

Pheasant, as well as all other game birds, should not be overcooked. The pheasant adapts well to sauces because of its distinctive flavor, and its tendency to dryness.

Some of the methods of preparation that have been well received at our annual game dinners and by our many customers who enjoy wild game, are as follows.

PAN-FRIED PHEASANT

WHAT'S NEEDED:

2 eggs
2 Tablespoons milk
salt and pepper
1 pheasant, quartered and disjointed
1 cup all purpose breading (seasoned coating mix)
1/2 cup butter
1/2 cup hot water
2 chicken bouillon cubes

HERE'S HOW:

1. Beat eggs and milk with a fork until well mixed.
2. Season pheasant with salt and pepper and dip in egg-milk mixture.
3. Coat with thin breading coating.
4. Heat butter in heavy fry pan. Add pheasant and brown over medium heat.
5. Add 1/2 cup hot water to the pan (be careful, this may splatter).
6. Add bouillon cubes, cover and simmer at low heat for 50-60 minutes or until tender.

Note:

For more crisp pheasant prepare steps 1 through 4, remove from fry pan and place on baking sheet and bake at 350 degrees for 1 hour, or until tender.

2 Servings

Baked Pheasant with Brandied Peach Glaze

WHAT'S NEEDED:

1 pheasant (the bird may be left whole or split in half)
1/4 cup butter, melted
salt and pepper
paprika
aluminum foil

HERE'S HOW:

1. Brush pheasant with butter. Season with salt and pepper, dust with paprika.
2. Wrap tightly in foil, bake at 350 degrees 1 hour or until pheasant is tender.
3. Make glaze.

Brandied Peach Glaze

WHAT'S NEEDED:

4 halves of yellow cling peaches
1/4 cup liquid from canned peaches
1/2 cup sugar
1-1/2 ounces Brandy
dash of cinnamon or nutmeg

HERE'S HOW:

1. Place the peaches, liquid, sugar, Brandy and cinnamon or nutmeg in blender and blend thoroughly.
2. Place in sauce pan and heat to boiling. Remove from heat.
3. Remove pheasant from foil and brush with glaze. Return to oven for 5 minutes; repeat until well glazed.

2 Servings

PHEASANT NORMANDIE

This is one of the truly great gourmet dishes of France. Here we have made it very easy to prepare by eliminating some of the involved and time consuming procedures.

WHAT'S NEEDED:

>   salt and pepper
>   2 pheasants, split in half
>   butter
>   paprika
>   4 cups beef stock (see index)
>   1 teaspoon tomato paste
>   2 apples, skin on, cored and cut into 1 inch cubes
>   1/2 cup dry white wine
>   2 ounces Calvados Brandy
>   3 beef bouillon cubes
>   3 green onions or shallots, diced
>   cornstarch or arrowroot and water paste (optional)

HERE'S HOW:

1. Salt and pepper the pheasant, then dust with paprika.
2. Brown the birds in butter.
3. Drain any surplus butter and add the rest of the ingredients except cornstarch or arrowroot paste.
4. Cook covered, over medium heat for 45 minutes.
5. If desired, the sauce may be thickened slightly with a paste made of cornstarch or arrowroot and water.

Note:
This is an excellent dish served on a bed of wild rice.

4 Servings

PHEASANT IN ASPIC

WHAT'S NEEDED:

> 1 cooked pheasant (boiled)
> 1 quart liquid (use pheasant stock plus water)
> 2 ounces powdered unflavored gelatin
> yellow food color (or any color you prefer)
> 3 hard boiled eggs, coarsely diced
> 8 pitted black olives, diced
> 8 stuffed green olives, diced
> 1 celery heart, diced very fine
> 1/2 teaspoon salt

HERE'S HOW:

> 1. Bone and dice meat from cooked pheasant. Boil one quart of liquid (stock and water), add the gelatin.

2. Remove from heat and add a few drops of coloring.
3. Cool completely.
4. Add the eggs, olives, celery, salt and meat.
5. Pour into an oiled 2 quart mold and refrigerate.
6. Unmold, slice and serve with crackers or breads.

10-12 Servings

ROAST PHEASANT WITH STUFFING

WHAT'S NEEDED:

1 pheasant, split in half
1/4 cup butter, melted
salt and pepper
paprika
Basic Stuffing (see index)
aluminum foil

HERE'S HOW:

1. Brush pheasant with butter. Season with salt and pepper and dust with paprika.
2. Fill small baking casserole or pan half full of stuffing.
3. Place seasoned pheasant on top of stuffing. Cover with foil tent and place in 350 degree oven for 1 hour or until tender.
4. Remove foil for last 10-15 minutes allowing pheasant to brown slightly.

2 Servings

Pheasant Soup with Wild Rice

WHAT'S NEEDED:

- 2 pheasants
- 1 medium onion, peeled
- 3 ribs celery
- 2 teaspoons salt
- 3/4 teaspoon pepper
- 1 bay leaf
- 2 gallons water
- 1/4 cup dry Sherry
- 2 cups cooked wild rice

HERE'S HOW:

1. Place the pheasants, onion, celery, salt, pepper and bay leaf in a pot with 2 gallons of water and bring to a boil.
2. Reduce heat and allow to simmer until the water is reduced to 1-1/2 quarts.
3. Remove the pheasants, debone and dice the meat into 1/4 inch cubes.
4. Strain the remaining stock through a sieve.
5. Add the diced pheasant, Sherry and cooked wild rice to the stock.

Note:

A teaspoon of chicken bouillon, a couple of diced canned pimentos and a dash of yellow food coloring will enhance the flavor and appearance of this soup. Can also serve with cooked white rice, noodles or spaetzle instead of wild rice.

Makes 3 quarts

Pheasant Marengo

WHAT'S NEEDED:

2 pheasants, quartered
salt and pepper
2 teaspoons butter
4 ounces whole button mushrooms
2 green onions, diced fine
1/2 clove garlic, diced extremely fine
1 cup white wine
8 ounces tomato sauce
1 cup chicken stock or 1 cup of hot water and 2 chicken
  bouillon cubes

HERE'S HOW:

1. Season pheasant with salt and pepper.
2. Saute in butter until golden brown.
3. In a separate pan, saute mushrooms, green onions and garlic until golden brown.
4. Add white wine, tomato sauce and chicken stock.
5. Pour this sauce over the pheasant.
6. Cover and simmer for about 45 minutes, or until tender.

4 Servings

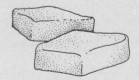

Pheasant in Red Wine Sauce

WHAT'S NEEDED:

1 pheasant, split in half
salt and pepper
paprika
1/4 cup butter or cooking oil
6 large mushrooms, preferably fresh
1 small onion, peeled, cut in half
2 ribs celery
1/2 pint Beef Stock (see index)
1 cup red Burgundy wine
3 beef bouillon cubes
cornstarch or arrowroot and water to form paste

HERE'S HOW:

1. Season the pheasant with salt and pepper, dust with paprika, saute in butter or cooking oil until golden brown.
2. Remove pheasant from pan and saute mushrooms, onion and celery until slightly browned.
3. Drain all butter or oil from pan and place pheasant in pan with celery, onion and mushrooms, cover with beef stock, add the wine and bouillon cubes. Simmer covered over low heat for 1 hour or until pheasant is tender.
4. Thicken the sauce with the paste made of cornstarch or arrowroot and water. Simmer on very low heat for 10 minutes and serve the pheasant covered with sauce.

2 Servings

There are two types of ptarmigan, Willow and Rock. Both are native to the Arctic and sub-Arctic regions. Both are strong tasting, dark meated birds. There are two options to be exercised in the care and preparation of this bird. Option Number 1: Give the bird to your favorite taxidermist. Option Number 2: Follow the instructions listed below and hope that the result will be edible.

BAKED PTARMIGAN WITH BRANDIED APRICOT SAUCE

WHAT'S NEEDED:

> **4 parboiled ptarmigan**
> **salt and pepper**
> **butter**
> **Brandied Apricot Sauce (see index)**

HERE'S HOW:

1. Place the ptarmigan in enough cold salted water to cover.
2. Bring to a boil.
3. Remove from heat and drain immediately.
4. Place in a baking dish, brush with butter and season with salt and pepper.
5. Place in a 350 degree oven for 25-30 minutes.
6. While baking, prepare Brandied Apricot Sauce.
7. Remove from oven and brush with sauce.
8. Reduce heat to 275 degrees and return birds to oven for 30 minutes.
9. Brush with sauce a couple of times at ten minute intervals.

4 Servings

FRIED BREAST OF PTARMIGAN

WHAT'S NEEDED:

4 whole ptarmigan breasts, skinned and deboned
   (8 fillets)
1/2 teaspoon salt
1/4 teaspoon black pepper
egg wash: 2 eggs, 2 Tablespoons milk, beaten together
1/2 cup cracker meal
1/2 cup butter
2 Tablespoons Cointreau or Triple-Sec

HERE'S HOW:

1. Blanch by placing the breasts of ptarmigan in enough cold water to cover them. Bring to a boil and immediately remove from heat. Do not cook.
2. Salt and pepper the breasts. Dip them in the egg wash.
3. Roll the breasts in cracker meal.
4. Place 1/2 cup butter in a heavy fry pan. Add the ptarmigan and the Cointreau and cook covered for about 20-25 minutes until the birds are tender.

4 Servings

DEEP FRIED QUAIL

WHAT'S NEEDED:

> 2 quail per person
> flour
> onion salt
> garlic powder
> salt and pepper
> paprika
> oil for deep frying

HERE'S HOW:

1. Season the quail lightly and dust with paprika.
2. Dip quail in flour.
3. Deep fry at 350 degrees for about 4 minutes.

Note:

Remember eye appeal and color. Decorate your plate with mandarin oranges. Arrange them in flower petal shapes.

1 Serving

QUAIL TERIYAKI

WHAT'S NEEDED:

8 quail (allowing 2 per person)
2 quarts boiling water
1/2 cup butter, melted
1/3 cup teriyaki or soy sauce
1 teaspoon garlic powder
1 teaspoon onion salt
1/4 teaspoon salt
1/4 teaspoon black pepper

HERE'S HOW:

1. Split the quail down the back, removing the neck.
2. Break the breastbone from the inside.
3. Pound the quail lightly with a cleaver to flatten.
4. Place in boiling water and boil for 15 minutes. Remove quail from the water.
5. Make teriyaki butter by mixing the remaining ingredients.
6. Dip the quail in the teriyaki butter, fry in a hot buttered pan for about one minute on both sides until browned.

4 Servings

STUFFED QUAIL

WHAT'S NEEDED:

Basic Stuffing (see index)
2 quail per person
1/4 cup butter
salt and pepper
paprika

Note:

In stuffing quail let your good taste dictate the stuffing mixture. The opportunities here are limitless to indulge the wildest tastes. To the Basic Stuffing found in the index, you can add darn near anything. Try fruit chunks, dates, browned sausage, apples, nuts, chopped fresh oysters, water chestnuts or anything else that comes to mind.

HERE'S HOW:

1. Stuff the quail with the stuffing of your choice.
2. In a buttered baking dish place a layer of stuffing at least an inch and a half deep.
3. Brush the quail with butter, season with salt and pepper, dust with paprika and arrange the quail in the baking dish on top of the stuffing.
4. Bake in a 350 degree oven for about 25-30 minutes. Do not overcook.

1 Serving

GLAZED BOBWHITE QUAIL WITH WILD RICE PATTIES

WHAT'S NEEDED:

> 2 quail per person
> salt and pepper
> 1/4 cup butter
> 1/2 cup crabapple jelly
> juice of 1/4 lemon
> 1 ounce Galliano

HERE'S HOW:

1. Saute seasoned quail in butter. Place in casserole.
2. Mix remaining ingredients in sauce pan over low heat.
3. Brush quail with this glaze and place in 325 degree oven covered for 30 minutes, uncovered last 15 minutes.
4. Serve with Wild Rice Patty (see index).

1 Serving

PAN-FRIED QUAIL

WHAT'S NEEDED:

2 quail per person
salt and pepper
garlic powder
ground nutmeg
egg wash: 1 egg, 1 Tablespoon milk, beaten together
1/2 cup flour
butter for frying
Brandied Peach Sauce (see index)

HERE'S HOW:

1. Season quail to taste with salt and pepper, very sparingly.
2. Add dash of garlic powder and dash of nutmeg.
3. Dip seasoned quail in egg wash.
4. Dredge with flour.
5. Pan fry in butter over medium heat until golden brown and tender. Do not overcook.
6. Serve on a bed of wild rice and top with Brandied Peach Sauce.

1 Serving

BROCHETTE OF SQUAB

WHAT'S NEEDED:

8 breasts of squab (allowing 2 per person)

1 cup wild rice

3 cups salted water

salt and pepper

1 whole (canned) pimento, diced coarsely

1/4 cup sliced or chopped macadamia nuts

1/4 cup canned mushrooms, stems and pieces

2 Tablespoons butter

2 egg whites

egg wash: 2 whole eggs, 2 Tablespoons milk, beaten
together

1 cup all purpose breading (seasoned coating mix)

chive and onion flavored sour cream

HERE'S HOW:

1. Split the squab down the back bone. Remove the back bone, neck and legs. Remove the wings, and remove all bones from the breast.
2. Flatten the breast with a cleaver.
3. Prepare the rice dressing by boiling the rice in the salted water until tender and fluffed.
4. Season to taste with salt and pepper.
5. Mix the cooked rice, macadamia nuts, mushrooms and pimento.
6. Add the butter and season with salt and pepper to taste.
7. Stuff the breast with wild rice mixture (about 2 ounces).
8. Pound the edges lightly to seal them, brush with the egg whites and freeze.
9. Whip the two eggs and 2 Tablespoons of milk to form an egg wash.

10. Dip the frozen birds in the egg wash and then in breading. Repeat if necessary, to form a good seal.
11. Place on a baking sheet. Brush lightly with butter and bake at 350 degrees for approximately one hour.
12. Serve with chive and onion flavored sour cream.

4 Servings

SUPREME OF SQUAB

WHAT'S NEEDED:

1 whole deboned breast of squab per person
salt and pepper
1/2 clove garlic, diced to a pulp
1 green onion, diced fine
2 ounces bleu cheese
1 egg white, beaten
egg wash: 1 egg, 1 Tablespoon milk, beaten together
1/2 cup all purpose breading (seasoned coating mix)

HERE'S HOW:

1. Stuff seasoned breast with a mixture of garlic, green onion and bleu cheese. Brush entire bird with beaten egg white, so as to seal edges.
2. Freeze and repeat the brushing.
3. Dip in egg wash. Coat with breading and refreeze. Repeat as necessary to form a good seal.
4. It is advisable to brown in a deep fryer, then bake for 45-60 minutes in a 375 degree oven.

1 Serving

FRIED BREAST OF WILD TURKEY

WHAT'S NEEDED:

    1 whole deboned turkey breast (2 fillets)
    salt and pepper
    egg wash: 2 eggs, 2 Tablespoons milk, beaten together
    1 cup all purpose breading or cracker meal
    1/2 cup butter
    1 ounce white wine

HERE'S HOW:

1. Season the turkey breasts with salt and pepper.
2. Dip in the egg wash.
3. Dip in the breading.
4. Place about 1/4 inch of butter in a heavy fry pan and saute the breasts until browned on both sides.
5. Reduce the heat, cover and simmer for 25 minutes.
6. Add the white wine.
7. Cover and simmer for 15 minutes or until meat is tender.

Note:

To add color to your plate take jellied cranberry sauce and slice 1/4 inch thick and use cookie cutters to cut out designs in any shape desired.

4-6 Servings

SMOKED TURKEY AND CHEESE SANDWICH

WHAT'S NEEDED:

1/2 pound soft butter

3 Tablespoons prepared mustard

1-1/2 Tablespoons poppy seeds

1 teaspoon Worcestershire sauce

1 onion, grated

hamburger buns

2 pounds smoked wild turkey, sliced thinly

Swiss cheese slices

HERE'S HOW:

1. Mix the first 5 ingredients and spread on both sides of buns.
2. Place sliced turkey and cheese on buns and wrap in foil.
3. Heat at 400 degrees for 10 minutes.

16 Servings

WILD TURKEY WITH WILD RICE STUFFING

WHAT'S NEEDED:

1 whole (8-10 pound) wild turkey
Basic Stuffing (see index)
2 cups cooked wild rice
1/4 cup melted butter
1/2 teaspoon oregano

HERE'S HOW:

1. Mix 3 cups Basic Stuffing with the wild rice, melted butter and oregano.
2. Stuff the bird cavity with the mixture.
3. Brush turkey with mixture of:
   1/4 cup melted butter
   1/4 teaspoon salt
   1/4 teaspoon pepper
   1/4 teaspoon oregano
4. Place in baking pan, cover with foil tent and bake in medium oven, 350 degrees for 15 minutes per pound.
5. Thirty minutes before removing from oven, remove foil and continue baking until brown.
6. Brush occasionally with seasoned butter mixture.

4-6 Servings

WELLINGTON OF WILD TURKEY

WHAT'S NEEDED:

- 1/4 cup chicken liver pate
- 1/2 ounce Cognac
- 1 recipe of Wellington Pastry (see index)
- 2 deboned wild turkey breast fillets, tied to form tubular shapes
- 1/4 cup butter
- 2 egg whites (left over from the Wellington Pastry recipe)

HERE'S HOW:

1. Mix the chicken liver pate and Cognac and spread on the pastry to a thickness of 1/8 to 1/4 inch.
2. Saute the shaped, tied turkey breasts in 1/4 cup butter until brown.
3. Remove the turkey breasts from the pan, allow to cool. Remove the ties and roll the turkey breasts in the Wellington Pastry. (CAUTION: Do not use more than one thickness of pastry except for a seal.)
4. Whip the egg whites with a fork and brush the Wellington with this mixture.
5. Place in a fairly hot oven (375 degrees) for approximately 1 hour and 15 minutes, until the pastry is a golden brown.

4-6 Servings

Upland Gamebird Wings

WHAT'S NEEDED:

1/4 cup soy sauce

1/4 cup dry Sherry

1/2 cup water

2 Tablespoons brown sugar

1 teaspoon medium dry mustard

2 green onions, diced

16-20 bird wings

HERE'S HOW:

1. In a large pan combine all ingredients, including wings.
2. Simmer covered for 40 minutes and uncovered for 15 minutes.
3. Serve hot or cold.

4-5 Servings

BIG GAME

Big Game Field Facts

More game is probably made unpalatable by improper care and handling in the field, than by any form of cookery. Big game (moose, bear, elk, deer and all red meated animals) should be eviscerated (gutted) immediately after determining that the animal is indeed dead. This precaution is absolutely essential, as wounded animals are sometimes a bit feisty.

Immediate field care is essential to insure the high quality of the game. These are the general procedures for rough field dressing. The first step is to remove all viscera (internal organs) by inserting a sharp knife through the flesh just above the hard boney section of the brisket and making an incision the length of the animal, to the pelvic area. Use your forefinger and index finger as guides, being careful not to pierce the abdominal sac. Once the incision has been made, gently pull out the viscera and save the liver. The colon may be removed by incising around the anus. Use a small hatchet to split the brisket for easy access to the diaphragm, lungs and heart. Cut the windpipe as high as possible in the neck area. At this point, most of your hard work is done. Water will not hurt the meat and water or snow may be used to remove as much of the blood, debris or excrement as possible.

Large animals are usually skinned on the ground and quartered. If small enough the animal should be hung, head up and then skinned from the shoulders down. The body cavity should be propped open and allowed to cool. Cold weather presents no problem, but warm weather may bring flies and other insects. To avoid this, a coarse cloth or netting material should be used to cover the animal, being sure that air can circulate. Needless to say, in warm weather it is absolutely essential that the meat be moved to a cool place as quickly as possible. When transporting home, a car-top carrier or a trailer is preferable to transporting in a closed trunk or on the warm hood of a vehicle.

Some game meats, particularly moose and big cats, have a tendency to be flaccid and should be hung in a refrigerated area for several days to allow meat to "firm up". Having listened to thirty years of violent disagreement among knowledgeable hunters on the proper method of cutting game, I can only advise that if you have the tools and the know-how to cut your own meat, you are now ready to do so. If you have the tools, but not the know-how and insist on doing it yourself, any meat market can supply you with a meat cutting guide. If you have neither the skill nor the tools, but are imbued with vast wisdom or a certain modicum of common sense, take it to your favorite butcher and let him handle it.

ANTELOPE, GOAT AND SHEEP

I'm grouping these animals together and treating them as one family. The taste and texture are so similar that the same basic directions apply in their preparation. All of these game meats are of delicate flavor and should not be overcooked. These animals should be treated the same as domestic lamb.

PAN FRIED CHOPS OF ANTELOPE, GOAT OR SHEEP

WHAT'S NEEDED:

> 6 chops or sliced round of game
> oregano
> salt and pepper
> garlic powder
> 1/3 cup flour
> 1/2 cup butter
> lemon wedges

HERE'S HOW:

1. Season meat to taste with salt, pepper, oregano and garlic powder. Dredge with flour.
2. Fry in butter over medium heat in a heavy covered pan. Turn once frying 3 minutes per side or until medium done.
3. Serve with lemon wedges.

3-4 Servings

Antelope, Goat or Sheep Shish Ke-Bab

WHAT'S NEEDED:

1 pound game meat, cut in 1" cubes
1 fresh green pepper, cut in 1" cubes
24 large, fresh or canned mushrooms
canned pimento, cut in 1" sections
12 skewers
1 can small whole boiled onions

FOR MARINADE:

1 to 1-1/2 cups cooking oil
2 cloves garlic, peeled and coarsely chopped
2 ounces dry white wine
1/2 teaspoon salt
1/4 teaspoon pepper
1/4 onion, coarsely chopped
1/8 teaspoon oregano
juice of 1/4 fresh lemon

HERE'S HOW:

1. Alternate chunks of meat, green pepper, mushrooms, pimento and onion on the skewers, until 3 or 4 meat chunks have been used. (Press firmly, don't leave spaces on the skewers.)
2. Mix all marinade ingredients in glass dish.
3. Place the skewered shish ke-bab in dish and refrigerate 2-3 hours turning occasionally.
4. Broil under broiler 8 minutes on each side or to the desired doneness.

4-6 Servings

Marinated Chops of Antelope, Goat or Big Horn Sheep

WHAT'S NEEDED:

>2/3 cup fresh lemon juice
>3 Tablespoons grated lemon rind
>1-1/2 Tablespoons tarragon
>1 cup Galliano
>8 chops
>1/2 cup butter or cooking oil

HERE'S HOW:

1. Mix the lemon juice, lemon rind, tarragon and Galliano together.
2. Add the chops, cover and refrigerate for 4 or 5 hours, turning occasionally.
3. Remove the chops from marinade, pan fry in butter or grill to the desired degree of doneness, turning once.

3-4 Servings

Big Game Irish Stew

WHAT'S NEEDED:

>2 pounds antelope, goat or sheep, diced into 1" cubes
>1 pound tiny whole potatoes, peeled
>5 carrots, peeled and sliced into 1" chunks
>1 medium onion, chopped coarsely
>3 ribs celery, cut into 1" chunks
>1 teaspoon salt
>1/4 teaspoon pepper
>2 (8 ounce) cans tomato sauce

HERE'S HOW:

1. Blanch the meat by placing it in a pan, covering with cold water and bringing to a boil. Remove from heat. Drain and rinse thoroughly.
2. Place the meat and remaining ingredients in a kettle and cover with hot water.
3. Bring to a boil. Cover the kettle and reduce heat to simmer.
4. Allow to simmer 1 hour or until vegetables are tender.

4-6 Servings

MEDALLIONS OF ANTELOPE, GOAT OR SHEEP WITH GLAZED PINEAPPLE RINGS

WHAT'S NEEDED:

2 tenderloins of antelope, goat or sheep
1 large can pineapple rings, save juice for sauce
salt and pepper
oregano
flour
butter
sugar

HERE'S HOW:

1. Cut the defatted tenderloins into one inch chunks.
2. Drain the pineapple and allow to dry on absorbent paper towels.
3. Season the chunks (medallions) with salt, pepper and oregano.
4. Roll in flour and fry at moderate heat in butter for about three minutes per side in a covered pan.
5. Dip the pineapple rings in sugar, then in flour.
6. Grill or pan fry the pineapple rings in butter until golden brown.
7. When the meat is done to your taste, remove and top each piece with a pineapple ring.

Note:
May be served with Orange Pineapple Sauce (see index).

Number served depends upon size of tenderloin

ROAST LEG OF ANTELOPE, GOAT OR SHEEP

WHAT'S NEEDED:

1 (6-7 pound) hind leg of game
1 clove garlic, peeled and sliced in very thin slivers
1-1/2 teaspoon salt
1/2 teaspoon pepper
1/2 teaspoon oregano or ground rosemary
paprika
juice of 1/2 fresh lemon
mint jelly

HERE'S HOW:

1. Pierce the meat with a large cooking fork at 1'' intervals. Insert the very thin garlic slivers into the holes.
2. Season with salt, pepper, oregano or rosemary. Dust with paprika.
3. Bake at 350-375 degrees for 40-45 minutes until medium or until meat thermometer registers 175 degrees.
4. Baste occasionally with lemon juice.
5. Serve hot or cold, with mint jelly.

6-8 Servings

CROWN RACK OF ANTELOPE, ROCKY MOUNTAIN GOAT OR SHEEP

WHAT'S NEEDED:

> 1 crown rack of antelope, goat or sheep
> aluminum foil
> 1/2 cup cooking oil
> 1 teaspoon salt
> 1/2 teaspoon pepper
> 1/2 teaspoon garlic powder
> 1 quart Basic Stuffing (see index)
> 2 apples, peeled, cored and diced into 1/2'' chunks
> 3/4 teaspoon curry powder
> spiced crabapples, melon balls, or paper frills
> prepared mint sauce or jelly

HERE'S HOW:

1. Ask your favorite butcher to prepare the crown rack for you using the 7 primary ribs. These should be skewered together securely so as to form a circle or crown.

2. Remove the membrane from the ribs down to the meaty section.

3. Cover the exposed bone area with foil to prevent its burning in the oven.

4. Brush the exposed portion of the crown roast with cooking oil and season with salt, pepper and garlic powder.

5. Stuff the center of the roast with Basic Stuffing to which you will have added the diced apples and curry powder.

6. Place on a greased rimmed baking sheet and bake in a 375 degree oven for about one hour.

7. Remove the roast from oven and remove the foil from the bones. You may want to decorate these bones with spiced crabapples, melon balls or paper frills.

8. When serving, simply slice between the rib bones, using one section per person. Serve with mint sauce or jelly.

3-4 Servings

Big Horn Sheep Shish Ke-Bab

WHAT'S NEEDED:

1/2 cup mint jelly
1/4 teaspoon oregano
1/4 teaspoon powdered bay leaf
1/2 clove garlic, diced to a pulp
1/4 teaspoon salt
1/4 teaspoon pepper
2 teaspoons fresh lemon juice
4 double-cut boned chops
cherry tomatoes
1 onion, cut in 1'' cubes
large fresh or canned mushroom caps
1 green pepper, cut in 1'' squares
salt and pepper
1/4 cut butter, melted

HERE'S HOW:

1. Prepare a paste with the first 7 ingredients.
2. Brush double-cut chop with this paste, covering all surfaces.
3. Place a cherry tomato, a cube of onion, a mushroom cap and a square of green pepper on a skewer.
4. Fold the chop into a roll and place it on the skewer and repeat vegetables on other side.
5. Season with salt and pepper.
6. Place on a pan or rack under the broiler, turning occasionally and basting with butter until the meat is about medium (20-25 minutes).

Note:
Other big game meat may be used in this recipe.

4 Servings

BEAR

Lucky is the hunter who brings home a bear of any kind, be it a native black, brown, or grizzly, or the "King" of them all, the polar bear. Terrified is the lady who is handed several hundred pounds of bear meat and asked to prepare it. (Be of strong heart, my dear, bear meat is rich, tender and delicious.)

Note: Complete removal of *all* fat is necessary, even before freezing. Never use the liver of the polar bear as it is toxic and dangerous. Bear meat must be cooked well-done as the bear may be a carrier of trichinosis.

BEAR ROAST

WHAT'S NEEDED:

> 1 (5 pound) roast (all fat removed)
> 1 Tablespoon salt
> 1/2 teaspoon pepper
> 5 strips bacon or salt pork
> 1 medium onion, sliced
> 2 ribs celery, cut in 3" pieces

HERE'S HOW:

1. Place roast in pan and season with salt and pepper.
2. Lay 5 bacon strips or salt pork on roast.
3. Cover with onion and celery.
4. Bake covered at 350 degrees for 3 hours or until meat is well done. To brown, uncover last 1/2 hour.

5-6 Servings

PAN FRIED BEAR STEAKS

WHAT'S NEEDED:

>1/2 onion, medium sliced
>1/2 cup vinegar
>1/2 cup water
>1/2 cup vegetable oil
>1 Tablespoon whole pickling spice
>1 Tablespoon salt
>4 bear steaks, 1" thick
>butter or cooking oil for frying
>salt and pepper

HERE'S HOW:

1. Make a marinade of onion, vinegar, water, vegetable oil, pickling spice and salt.
2. Place steaks in a bowl, add marinade and refrigerate covered for 24 hours. Turn meat occasionally.
3. Remove from marinade and pan fry in butter or cooking oil until well done on each side.
4. Season to taste with salt and pepper.

4 Servings

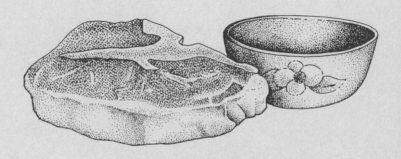

STROGANOFF OF BEAR

WHAT'S NEEDED:

3/4 cup butter

2 pounds bear round, cubed into 1'' squares (all fat removed)

6 ounce jar of whole button mushrooms

1/4 cup white wine

1/4 cup vinegar

1 pint Brown Gravy (see index)

1 cup sour cream

salt and pepper

boiled rice or noodles

HERE'S HOW:

1. Place 1/2 cup butter, the cubed bear meat and mushrooms in a heavy skillet and saute until brown.
2. Mix the white wine and vinegar and boil for 5 minutes.
3. Heat the Brown Gravy and add the white wine and vinegar mixture.
4. Add the sour cream to the hot gravy mixture stirring constantly.
5. Add the remaining 1/4 cup of unmelted butter. Stir well.
6. Drain all butter from the bear and mushrooms.
7. Pour sauce over the bear and mushrooms.
8. Salt and pepper to taste.
9. Serve hot over cooked rice or noodles. **4-6 Servings**

Bear Stew Espagnole

WHAT'S NEEDED:

3 pounds bear meat, cut in 1'' cubes
1 Tablespoon salt
1/4 cup shortening
2 cloves garlic, minced to a pulp
1/2 cup diced celery
1 onion, sliced
1 green pepper, diced
1 cup dry white wine
1 (6 ounce) can tomato paste
2 cups canned tomatoes, crushed
dash of Tabasco
1/2 teaspoon salt
1/4 teaspoon black pepper

HERE'S HOW:

1. Season the bear meat with salt to taste and pan fry in shortening until browned.
2. Saute the garlic, celery, onion and green pepper. Simmer until onion is golden brown.
3. Add remaining ingredients and mix well.
4. Cover and simmer 30 minutes or until meat is well done.

4-6 Servings

Boiled Round of Bear with Horseradish Sauce

WHAT'S NEEDED:

1 (4 pounds) round of bear, boned and completely
   defatted
cold water to cover
1 medium onion, cut in quarters
2 large carrots, peeled
3 ribs celery, washed
1 bay leaf
1 whole clove
1/4 teaspoon coarsely ground pepper
1/2 teaspoon salt
Horseradish Sauce (see index)

HERE'S HOW:

1. Place the meat in a pan, cover with cold water.
2. Bring to a boil. After boiling for a few minutes, a scum will appear.
3. Remove the scum. Add the vegetables and seasonings.
4. Reduce the heat and simmer, covered, about 1½ to 2 hours.
5. Slice meat thinly against the grain and serve hot with Horseradish Sauce.

4 Servings

WHOLE ROAST WILD BOAR
A LA COLLINS

WHAT'S NEEDED:

> 2 cloves garlic, peeled
> 1 wild boar (125 pound), skinned (if it won't fit into your oven, cut it in half just behind the rib cage)
> 1/2 cup cooking oil
> salt and pepper
> 1 can condensed consomme madrilene
> 2 (16 ounce) cans pineapple rings, drained
> 2 whole fresh pineapples
> whole spiced crabapples or canned spiced crabapple rings
> 2 bunches fresh parsley
> Cumberland Sauce (see index)

HERE'S HOW:

1. Cut garlic in very thin slices.
2. Puncture the boar at 3 inch intervals with large cooking fork and insert a sliver of garlic into each puncture.
3. Brush the animal with cooking oil. (This should be done occasionally during cooking also).
4. Season with salt and pepper. Place in a 325 degree oven, 15-20 minutes per pound or until boar is almost done, fork tender.
5. Remove from oven, brush on several coats of consomme and return to oven a few more minutes. (This will form a glaze which adds to the appearance.)
6. Place boar on large serving tray and prepare the pineapple rings as follows:

a. Dip pineapple rings in sugar, then flour.
b. Pan fry or grill in butter until golden brown.
c. Arrange the slices around the boar and over-lap a few slices along the boar's back.
d. Arrange the crabapples or slices on tray to add color.
e. The pineapple and crabapple centers may be filled with mint jelly or maraschino cherries.
f. Complete garnish with fresh whole pineapple and parsley and carve at table, serving the sliced meat with Cumberland Sauce.

30-50 Servings (if main course)
100-125 Servings (if other entrees)

BUFFALO

I've served buffalo at Collins Cafe many times and people do like it. I've talked to a number of people, among them men who have raised buffalo and older Indians knowledgeable in the lore of the past, when buffalo was the primary staple of life to them. They all agree that, regardless of age, sex or habitat, there is no such thing as tough buffalo meat. I can't argue with their theory. Buffalo is considered a sweet meat. Its flavor is definite, but not strong. Of all wild game, this is the one that could be easily accepted as a regular diet.

BUFFALO BURGER

The Buffalo burger probably has the greatest appeal, and here's how you make it. Allow 1/4 pound meat per burger.

WHAT'S NEEDED:

> **85% ground buffalo meat**
> **15% ground beef kidney suet**

HERE'S HOW:

1. Mix well. Shape into patties.
2. Pan fry or grill, turning once at which time they should be seasoned with salt and pepper, if desired, or any other favorite herbs and spices.
3. Serve on a bun or plain.

Pan Fried Buffalo Steak

This meat should be considered the same as prime beef but has a different flavor. Regardless of the cut of steak, the procedures are the same. Here's a take off on Steak Diane that is simple and tasty.

WHAT'S NEEDED:

> **Any number of buffalo steaks, 1/2'' to 1-1/2'' thick**
> **Per steak:**
>> **2 Tablespoons butter**
>> **1 green onion, diced**
>> **salt and pepper**
>> **1 Tablespoon Worcestershire sauce**
>> **1/4 ounce Brandy**

HERE'S HOW:

1. In a heavy fry pan, melt butter, add buffalo steak and green onion.
2. Cook over medium heat turning once, season with salt and pepper.
3. When done, remove meat from pan, add Worcestershire sauce and Brandy to browned butter and onion. (Be careful, this could flame!)
4. Pour this sauce over steak.

Roast Buffalo

Any cut of roast will do, standing rib, round, sirloin, sirloin tip, blade.

WHAT'S NEEDED:

1 (5 pound) roast
salt and pepper
2 Tablespoons paprika
1/2 onion, peeled and sliced
5 ribs celery, cut in 2'' pieces
4 carrots, peeled and cut in 2'' pieces
1/2 teaspoon pickling spice
1 tomato, sliced

HERE'S HOW:

1. Place roast in a baking pan and season with salt and pepper.
2. Add paprika for color.
3. Add all other ingredients and bake at 350 degrees for 2 hours and 15 minutes.

Note:
If you care to make a gravy or Au Jus, add 1 quart of water to the roast pan. Strain this stock and save it.

6-8 Servings

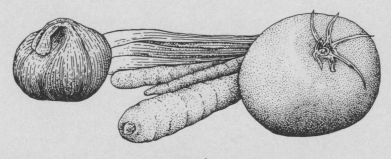

CARIBOU ROAST WITH BROWN GRAVY

WHAT'S NEEDED:

1 (3 pound) round (or any other cut, if preferred)
1/2 medium onion, sliced
3 cloves garlic, peeled
3 celery ribs
1/2 Tablespoon pickling spice
1/4 cup salt
1/2 Tablespoon pepper
3 Tablespoons paprika
1/2 pound slice of beef suet
1 cup tomato sauce
6 beef bouillon cubes
4 Tablespoons arrowroot or cornstarch
1/4 cup water

HERE'S HOW:

1. Place the roast in roasting pan.
2. Add onion, garlic, celery and pickling spice to pan.
3. Season with salt and pepper and dust with paprika.
4. Affix suet to roast with wood picks.
5. Bake, covered, 1 hour at 350 degrees.
6. Remove suet, add 1 quart water. Cover and continue to roast 1 hour.
7. Remove the roast from pan, strain remaining stock into a sauce pan. Add tomato sauce and bouillon cubes.
8. Heat this stock to a slow boil. Skim.
9. Make a paste of the arrowroot or cornstarch and water.
10. Add paste slowly to the stock, stirring constantly making a gravy to the desired consistency.

4-6 Servings

CARIBOU LIVER AND
HEART WITH ONIONS

WHAT'S NEEDED:

>1 liver and heart, thoroughly washed with veins removed
>salt and pepper
>flour
>butter
>1 onion, sliced 1/4'' thick

HERE'S HOW:

1. Slice the heart and liver about 1/4 inch thick.
2. Season with salt and pepper and dip in flour.
3. Saute onions in butter until half done, then add heart and liver slices. Fry until done.

6-8 Servings

BAKED STUFFED CARIBOU HEART

WHAT'S NEEDED:

1 heart
2 cups all purpose breading (seasoned coating mix)
1 rib celery, diced fine
1/2 medium onion, diced fine
1/4 teaspoon thyme
1/4 teaspoon poultry seasoning
1/2 teaspoon salt
1/4 teaspoon pepper
2 cups water

HERE'S HOW:

1. Trim off blood vessels, fat and cords from heart.
2. Mix stuffing mixture, celery, onion, thyme and seasoning.
3. Stuff cavity of heart with mixture.
4. Place heart on rack in roasting pan.
5. Season to taste with salt and pepper.
6. Add 2 cups water in bottom of roaster.
7. Cover and bake at 325 degrees for 2 hours or until tender.

2-4 Servings

Caribou Steaks or Chops

WHAT'S NEEDED:

steaks or chops, cut 1'' thick
butter
salt and pepper
MSG or Accent (optional)
fresh lemon wedges

HERE'S HOW:

1. Trim all fat and sinew from steaks or chops.
2. Preheat sufficient butter for frying in a heavy pan over medium heat.
3. Fry steaks or chops 4 minutes on one side. Turn, season to taste with salt, pepper and MSG or Accent.
4. Cook another 3 minutes.
5. As with all game meats, serve immediately. (A drop or two of fresh lemon juice applied at the table is sometimes desirable.)

Note:
Overcooking can destroy this delicate game meat.

Pepperoni

WHAT'S NEEDED:

10 pounds coarse ground caribou, elk, moose or venison
1/3 cup red pepper
1/3 cup black pepper
2/3 cup salt
1/4 cup sweet basil

HERE'S HOW:

1. Mix all ingredients well.
2. Form into bite-sized patties.
3. Pan fry, broil or grill.
4. Use what you need and freeze the rest.

Caribou Swiss Steak

WHAT'S NEEDED:

1 teaspoon salt

1 teaspoon black pepper

1 cup flour

1 (2 pound) caribou round steak, all fat removed

1/3 cup cooking oil

3 cups tomato sauce

1 clove garlic, diced extremely fine

1/2 onion, diced fine

1 rib celery, diced fine

HERE'S HOW:

1. Mix salt, pepper and flour together.
2. Tenderize steak by pounding with a meat tenderizer or mallet.
3. Dredge steak in seasoned flour.
4. Place oil in heavy fry pan, heat and add steak. Brown on both sides. Remove and place in baking pan.
5. Cover the steak with mixture of tomato sauce, garlic, onion and celery.
6. Pour over meat and bake covered at 350 degrees for 1-½ to 2 hours or until tender.

4 Servings

DEER / VENISON

Deer is probably the most commonly hunted big game animal in North America. Deer season usually occurs in the fall and is generally accompanied by certain infallible symptoms among hunters. A sudden appearance of guns, knives, bows and blaze orange clothing becomes evident and hunting stories take over fish tales.

DEER / VENISON BURGER

WHAT'S NEEDED:

> **5 pounds venison, all fat removed**
> **1/2 pound kidney suet**
> **salt and pepper**

HERE'S HOW:

1. Combine venison and suet and grind through regular grinder.
2. Season as you do your favorite burgers.
3. Shape into patties and pan fry or grill to desired degree of doneness.

6-8 Servings

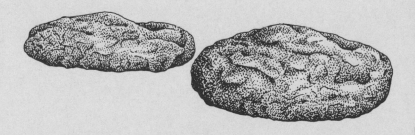

Deer/Venison Chili

WHAT'S NEEDED:

1-1/2 pounds dry red beans

1-1/2 gallons hot water

7 cloves garlic, peeled and diced to a pulp

1/2 large onion, diced very fine

2 pounds coarse ground venison (once only through your coarse grinder)

1/4 pound kidney suet, ground with venison

1/2 cup chili powder

1/3 cup salt

3 Tablespoons black pepper

HERE'S HOW:

1. Add the red beans to the hot water.
2. Bring to a boil and cook until beans are tender.
3. Add the garlic and onion to the ground meat and suet. Brown this mixture in a heavy skillet until the meat is completely cooked, 20 minutes or more.
4. Add all spices and seasonings to the cooked meat.
5. When beans are tender, add with remaining liquid to the meat.
6. Stir thoroughly and enjoy.

Note:

If you like the red hot Texas-style chili, add cayenne pepper (1/2 teaspoon or less).

6-8 Servings

Glazed Deer / Venison Meatloaf

WHAT'S NEEDED:

1/2 large onion, diced
2 ribs celery, diced
1 teaspoon salt
1/2 teaspoon pepper
2 pounds ground venison, all fat removed
2 beef bouillon cubes
1/2 cup hot water
3 eggs
3/4 cup cracker meal
Red Currant Glaze (see below)

HERE'S HOW:

1. Add onion, celery, salt and pepper to the ground venison.
2. Dissolve the 2 bouillon cubes in hot water and add to the vension mixture.
3. Add 3 whole eggs and cracker meal to the above, mix thoroughly.
4. Form the mixture into a loaf and place in greased loaf pan.
5. Make glaze by combining the following over low heat:
   1/4 cup red currant jelly
   1 Tablespoon Creme de Cassis liqueur
   1 teaspoon sugar
   2 Tablespoons water
6. Apply glaze to meatloaf with a pastry brush.
7. Preheat oven to 350 degrees and bake for 1 hour.

6-8 Servings

Deer/Venison Meat Sauce and Spaghetti

WHAT'S NEEDED:

2 pounds ground venison
3/4 cup chopped onion
3/4 cup green pepper
2 (12 ounce) cans tomato paste
2-1/2 cups hot water
1-1/2 cups plus 2 Tablespoons Burgundy wine
3 bay leaves, crushed
2 Tablespoons grated Parmesan cheese
1 teaspoon salt
3/4 teaspoon garlic powder
2 teaspoons sugar
1 teaspoon oregano
3/4 teaspoon ground rosemary
3/4 teaspoon basil
1 pound spaghetti, boiled in salted water

HERE'S HOW:

1. Brown meat, onion and green pepper over low heat until soft.
2. Drain excess juices.
3. Blend tomato paste, water, wine, cheese and seasonings into meat.
4. Simmer, covered, over low heat for 3 hours.
5. Serve over spaghetti.

8 Servings

Deer / Venison Steak with Herb Sauce

WHAT'S NEEDED:

1 small onion, diced very fine
2 Tablespoons butter
1 Tablespoon vinegar
12 whole peppercorns
1/2 teaspoon ham base or 2 ham flavored bouillon cubes
1 bay leaf
dash of thyme
1 teaspoon parsley flakes
1/2 pint Beef Stock (see index)
5 ounces red Port wine
1/4 cup red currant jelly
cornstarch or arrowroot and water
6 venison steaks, pan fried and kept warm
3 Tablespoons butter

HERE'S HOW:

1. Saute onion in butter until translucent.
2. Add the vinegar, peppercorns, ham base, bay leaf, thyme and parsley.
3. Cover and boil for 10 minutes.
4. Add the Beef Stock, wine and jelly.
5. Simmer 10 minutes more.
6. Strain.
7. Thicken with a paste of cornstarch or arrowroot and water.
8. Pour this sauce over venison steaks which have been pan fried in butter.

6 Servings

DEER / VENISON PAN FRIED STEAKS OR CHOPS

WHAT'S NEEDED:

> **2 Tablespoons butter**
> **1/2 dozen steaks or chops, 1'' thick**
> **salt and pepper**
> **garlic powder (optional)**
> **oregano (optional)**

HERE'S HOW:

1. Place butter in frying pan.
2. Preheat to medium heat and add venison.
3. Fry for 4 minutes or until browned. Turn and season with salt, pepper and garlic powder (or oregano) to taste.
4. Fry another 4 minutes.

4-6 Servings

DEER / VENISON ROAST

WHAT'S NEEDED:

1 clove garlic, diced to a pulp

1/2 teaspoon marjoram

1 teaspoon salt

1/2 teaspoon black pepper

1/2 cup cooking oil

1 (3 pound) roast of venison

HERE'S HOW:

1. Add garlic and other seasonings to the oil.
2. Let stand for 30 minutes.
3. Preheat oven to 350 degrees.
4. With a pastry brush coat the roast on all sides with the oil and seasoning mixture.
5. Bake for 25-30 minutes per pound depending on the degree of doneness desired. Baste often.

4-6 Servings

VENISON HAMBURGER CASSEROLE

WHAT'S NEEDED:

1 package refrigerated crescent rolls

1 pound ground venison

1/2 onion, diced

1 envelope taco seasoning

1 can refried beans

8 ounces sour cream

1 egg

4 ounces Cheddar cheese

HERE'S HOW:

1. Line a 9 x 13 pan with crescent rolls.
2. Brown ground venison and onion.
3. Combine taco seasoning, beans, sour cream, egg and cheese.
4. Place venison over crescent rolls and spread seasoned bean mixture over venison.
5. Bake for 30 minutes.

6-8 Servings

DEER / VENISON ROLL-UPS

WHAT'S NEEDED:

8 venison steaks, cut about 3/16" thick
salt and pepper
Basic Dressing (see index)
diced onion and celery (optional)
Brown Gravy (see index)

HERE'S HOW:

1. Roll out the venison steak and season lightly with salt and pepper.
2. Stuff with Basic Dressing, (to which you may add a small amount of fincly diccd onion and celery) and roll up. The finished piece should be about 2 inches in diameter.
3. Place roll-ups, open side down, in a lightly greased baking dish or pan.
4. Brown uncovered in 350 degree oven for about 20-25 minutes.
5. When meat is browned, cover roll-ups with Brown Gravy.
6. Return to oven, bake covered for approximately 30 minutes longer.

6-8 Servings

Deer/Vension Steak Milano

WHAT'S NEEDED:

> 1 cup Burgundy wine
> 1 clove garlic, minced extra fine
> 1 small onion, diced fine
> 1/4 teaspoon oregano
> 1 Tablespoon Worcestershire sauce
> 1 teaspoon salt
> 1/4 teaspoon pepper
> 2 teaspoons prepared mustard
> 1 Tablespoon sugar
> 2 Tablespoons butter
> 1 (2 - 2-1/2 pound) venison steak

HERE'S HOW:

1. Combine all ingredients, except steak, and heat until butter is thoroughly melted.
2. Pour sauce over steak and refrigerate several hours, turning meat frequently.
3. Remove steak from sauce and broil for 5 minutes on each side, basting the meat with the sauce.

4-6 Servings

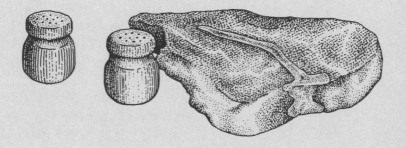

DEER/VENISON TONGUE MOUSSE

Cover a smoked tongue with cold salted water. Bring to a boil and simmer for 3-4 hours or until tender. Remove skin and grind meat.

WHAT'S NEEDED:

1 envelope Knox gelatin

1/4 cup cold water

3/4 cup beef bouillon

2 cups ground meat, as prepared above

1/4 cup mayonnaise

1 teaspoon prepared mustard

2 Tablespoons grated onion

1 Tablespoon minced parsley

1 Tablespoon lemon juice

1/4 teaspoon dill weed

1/4 cup cream, whipped

salt

cayenne

HERE'S HOW:

1. Soften gelatin in cold water and add to beef bouillon and heat until gelatin is dissolved.
2. Combine remaining ingredients and pour into mold and refrigerate (for 2 cups meat, use a 4 cup mold).
3. Serve on a bed of shredded lettuce with the following sauce: Combine 1 cup sour cream, 1 cup mayonnaise, 2 Tablespoons drained prepared horseradish (optional).

Note:
Serve as luncheon main course or as an hors d'oeuvre.

6-8 Luncheon Servings
(more as an hors d'oeuvre)

Smoked Venison Western Omelet

WHAT'S NEEDED:

12 slices bread
butter
2 pounds smoked venison, sliced very thin
1 pound grated Swiss cheese
2 cups milk
4 eggs, beaten
2 Tablespoons mustard
1 teaspoon Beau Monde seasoning
1 teaspoon Worcestershire sauce
2 dashes onion salt

HERE'S HOW:

1. Line a 9 x 13 baking dish with 6 slices of bread, buttered on both sides, crusts removed.
2. Top with half of the sliced venison and half of the grated cheese.
3. Layer again with remaining bread, venison and cheese.
4. Mix milk, eggs, mustard and seasonings together.
5. Pour mixture over meat and cheese, cover and refrigerate overnight.
6. Sprinkle with paprika and bake at 350 degrees for 1 hour.
7. Cool 10 minutes and serve.

8 Servings

Venison Sausage & Cheese

WHAT'S NEEDED:

2-1/2 cups seasoned croutons
2 cups sharp Cheddar cheese, grated
1-1/2 pounds venison sausage patties
4 eggs
2-1/2 cups milk
1/2 teaspoon salt - dash pepper
3/4 teaspoon dry mustard
1 can cream of mushroom soup
1/2 cup milk

HERE'S HOW:

1. Grease an 8 x 12 pan and place croutons on bottom. Sprinkle with 1-1/2 cups cheese.
2. Brown sausage patties, drain and place over cheese.
3. Beat eggs with 2-1/2 cups milk, salt, pepper and mustard. Pour over croutons, cover and refrigerate overnight.
4. Before baking the next morning, dilute mushroom soup with 1/2 cup milk and pour over sausage and eggs.
5. Sprinkle with remaining cheese.
6. Bake at 300 degrees for 1½ hours.

8 Servings

ELK

Elk or Wapiti, is considered by many to be the finest of game meat. The meat is tender, not strong or gamey flavored and can be handled exactly as beef. Since this meat is so simply prepared use the recipes already shown for venison, moose and caribou. But here are a few especially good for elk.

SWEET AND SOUR ELK

WHAT'S NEEDED:

>   3 pounds elk meat, diced into 1'' cubes
>   1/2 cup cornstarch
>   1 teaspoon salt
>   oil for deep frying
>   2 medium onions, diced medium
>   1 green pepper, diced medium
>   1/2 cup pineapple juice
>   3/4 cup sugar
>   1 cup white vinegar
>   1 cup soy sauce
>   1 teaspoon MSG or Accent (optional)
>   2 cups cooked rice (white or wild)
>   1 cup pineapple chunks, diced

HERE'S HOW:

1. Dip cubed elk in cornstarch seasoned with salt and pepper.
2. Deep fry until golden brown. Let drain.
3. Place remaining ingredients in large pan and simmer until green pepper is tender.
4. Add the meat and cook until liquid is reduced to a thick sauce.
5. Serve with rice.

4-6 Servings

Baked Short Rib of Elk

WHAT'S NEEDED:

3 pounds elk short ribs, cut in 2" lengths
cold water to cover
2 ribs celery, cut in 2" pieces
1 onion, peeled and chopped
3 cloves garlic, peeled
1/2 teaspoon pickling spice
3 Tablespoons salt
1 Tablespoon pepper
2 Tablespoons paprika

HERE'S HOW:

1. Place short ribs in sauce pan. Cover with cold water and bring to a boil to blanch.
2. Remove from heat, drain and rinse thoroughly with hot water.
3. Place the blanched ribs in a large roasting pan.
4. Add celery, onion, garlic and pickling spice.
5. Season the ribs with salt and pepper and sprinkle with paprika.
6. Place uncovered in 400 degree oven stirring occasionally so as to brown evenly, about 45 minutes.
7. Add enough hot water to cover ribs. Reduce heat to 325 degrees. Cover and return to oven and bake until tender, about 2 hours. Uncover for the last 15 minutes.

2 Servings

Elk Bourguignon

WHAT'S NEEDED:

1/4 pound diced salt pork

2 pounds elk chuck, rump or round, cut in 2'' cubes

1-1/2 teaspoons salt

freshly ground pepper

2 Tablespoons flour

1-1/2 cups dry red wine

1-1/2 cups water

herb bouquet: 1 carrot, sprig parsley, 1 bay leaf,
1/2 teaspoon thyme, 1 clove garlic. Place in
cheesecloth and tie with string

4 small onions, peeled and cut into 1'' pieces

1/2 pound fresh mushrooms or 2 (4 ounce) cans, sliced

parsley, minced

HERE'S HOW:

1. Fry salt pork until crisp, drain and save drippings.
2. Brown elk slowly on all sides in 2 Tablespoons of drippings.
3. Sprinkle with salt, pepper and flour, toss to coat evenly.
4. Place in a heavy 2 quart casserole, including salt pork.
5. Boil wine, water and herb bouquet together. Pour over meat.
6. Cover tightly and bake in 350 degree oven until tender, about 2 hours.
7. Skim off all fat.
8. Saute raw onions and mushrooms separately in a little of the fat for a few minutes.
9. Add onions to meat, bake an additional 30 minutes.
10. Add mushrooms, bake another 10 minutes.
11. Top with parsley.

4-6 Servings

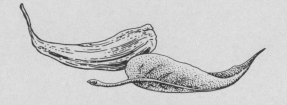

Elk Shish Ke-Bab

WHAT'S NEEDED:

1 large can mushroom caps (12)
1 large green pepper, cut into 1'' pieces
1 dozen cherry tomatoes
1 onion, cut into 1'' pieces
1 (2-3 pound) elk tenderloin, cut into 1'' pieces

FOR MARINADE:

6 ounces cooking oil
1/4 teaspoon garlic powder
1/4 teaspoon salt
1/4 teaspoon black pepper
1/4 teaspoon paprika
1 ounce Cognac

HERE'S HOW:

1. Mix marinade ingredients in sauce dish.
2. On a skewer place 1 mushroom cap, a section of green pepper, 1 cherry tomato, a chunk of onion and 1 cube of tenderloin. Repeat until skewer is full.
3. Place prepared skewer in marinade for 20 minutes.
4. Drain and broil on both sides until the meat reaches the desired degree of doneness.

4-6 Servings

Prime Rib of Elk, Au Jus

WHAT'S NEEDED:

1 (8-9 pound) standing rib of elk
1/2 pound suet or bacon
3 ribs celery
1 onion, cut in quarters
1/2 teaspoon pickling spice
4 cloves garlic, peeled
4 Tablespoons salt
1 Tablespoon pepper
3 teaspoons paprika
1-1/2 quarts water
6 beef bouillon cubes
4 ounces tomato puree

HERE'S HOW:

1. Remove fat from rib roast.
2. Place standing rib in roast pan, bone side down.
3. Affix suet or bacon to meat with wooden picks.
4. Add celery, onion, pickling spices and garlic.
5. Season with salt and pepper, dust with paprika.
6. Bake uncovered in 375 degree oven until brown, about 45 minutes.
7. Add water, reduce oven heat to 325 degrees and bake covered 10 minutes per pound.
8. Remove roast from pan. Remove fat from roast. Cut rib bones off or leave them on as desired.
9. Au Jus is prepared by straining the residue in the roast pan. (This should yield about 1 quart liquid.)
10. Reheat the quart of strained juice.
11. Dissolve bouillon cubes into hot liquid and add tomato puree. Bring to a boil.
12. Slice roast into desired number of slices. Serve covered with hot Au Jus.

6-8 Servings

Elk Meat Balls Italian Style

WHAT'S NEEDED:

- 1/2 onion, diced fine
- 2 ribs celery, diced fine
- 2 cloves garlic, diced to a pulp
- 1/4 cup vegetable oil
- 6 slices fresh bread, crusts removed and cubed
- 1/2 cup milk
- 2 pounds lean ground elk
- 2 eggs
- 2 Tablespoons grated Parmesan cheese
- 1/2 teaspoon parsley flakes
- 1/4 teaspoon oregano
- salt and pepper
- Spaghetti Sauce (see index)

HERE'S HOW:

1. Saute the onions, celery and garlic in oil.
2. In a large mixing bowl combine the bread and milk. Mix well.
3. Add cooled onions, celery, garlic and the remaining ingredients and season to taste.
4. Form the mixture into one inch balls.
5. Place the meat balls in a greased baking dish.
6. Bake covered at 350 degrees for about 20-25 minutes.
7. Serve with Spaghetti Sauce or your own favorite recipe.

**4-6 Servings
(more as an appetizer)**

ELK WELLINGTON

WHAT'S NEEDED:

3 ounces chicken liver pate, laced with 1/4 ounce of Brandy or Cognac.

1 recipe of Wellington Pastry (see index), rolled 1/8" thick

1 (2 pound) chunk of elk tenderloin, seared on all surfaces

3 egg whites, well beaten

Bordelaise Sauce (see index)

HERE'S HOW:

1. Spread the liver pate on the rolled out piece of Wellington Pastry.
2. Wrap the seared tenderloin in the pastry.
3. Seal and brush with egg whites to glaze.
4. Place in very hot oven, 400 degrees, for 35-40 minutes for medium rare.
5. Slice in 1 inch slices.
6. Serve with Bordelaise Sauce.

4-6 Servings

Note:

If you would like to personalize your dinner party — write your name or your guest's name out of pastry. Attach it to top of Elk Wellington by firmly pressing letters on the top and brushing with egg white.

MOOSE

The moose is the largest member of the deer family and can be hunted in Northern Minnesota, nearly all of Canada, and in many of the Western states and Alaska. I guess most hunters fantasize about laying their sights on this huge animal which can stand seven feet at the shoulder and weigh half a ton or more.

BARBECUED MOOSE RIBS

WHAT'S NEEDED:

>   moose ribs, cut into 5″ sections
>   salt and pepper
>   garlic powder (optional)
>   Wright's Condensed Liquid Smoke
>   Barbecue Sauce (see index), or use your favorite

HERE'S HOW:

1. Season ribs with salt, pepper and garlic powder.
2. Brush with Liquid Smoke.
3. Brown the ribs uncovered in medium oven at 350-375 degrees.
4. When browned, brush liberally with Barbecue Sauce.
5. Cover and bake at 325-350 degrees until tender. (An additional amount of Barbecue Sauce may be heated and served at the table with the ribs.)

Note:
This is sort of a quickie approach to the barbecue bit. If you have your own smoke house, smoker or whatever, ignore steps 1 and 2 and do your own thing.

4 Servings

LONDON HOUSE FILET OF MOOSE EN CROUTE

WHAT'S NEEDED:

1 (8 inch) chunk of moose tenderloin
butter or cooking oil
1 (8 ounce) can liver pate
1/2 ounce Brandy or Cognac
1/8 teaspoon salt
1/8 teaspoon coarse ground black pepper
2 green onions, finely diced
Wellington Pastry (see index)
2 egg whites, beaten
Bordelaise Sauce (see index)

HERE'S HOW:

1. Remove all fat and tissue from tenderloin.
2. Saute in a very hot pan with butter or cooking oil, until lightly browned on all surfaces. Do not allow to cook.
3. When tenderloin has cooled sufficiently to allow handling, slit it 3/4's of the way through horizontally.
4. Combine pate, Brandy, salt, pepper and onion. Mix well.
5. Stuff the cavity of the tenderloin with the seasoned pate and wrap with Wellington Pastry.
6. Brush all surfaces with beaten egg whites.
7. Place on baking sheet and bake at 400 degrees for 40 minutes for a medium rare filet.
8. Serve with Bordelaise Sauce.

6-8 Servings

MOOSE OR VENISON HAMBURGER

WHAT'S NEEDED:

> 3/4 pound ground meat
> 10 soda crackers, crushed
> 1/2 onion, finely diced
> salt and pepper

HERE'S HOW:

1. Mix all ingredients together in a bowl.
2. Shape into patties and pan fry or grill.
3. Season to taste, turning only once.

1-2 Servings

MOOSE MEATLOAF WITH WILD RICE

WHAT'S NEEDED:

> 1 pound ground moose meat
> 3 eggs
> 2 cups cooked wild rice (rice that has been boiled in salted water)
> 2 ribs celery, diced fine
> 1 small onion, diced fine
> 2 ounces canned mushrooms (stems and pieces)
> 1 teaspoon salt
> 1/4 teaspoon black pepper
> 2 ounces dry white wine

HERE'S HOW:

1. Mix all ingredients together thoroughly.
2. Form into loaf, place in baking pan.
3. Bake 1 hour at 350 degrees.

Note:

This is a very fine way to use moose meat or for that matter, venison, elk, caribou, or just plain cow.

4 Servings

Moose Hawaiian

WHAT'S NEEDED:

1 Tablespoon sugar

1 Tablespoon powdered ginger

1/2 clove garlic, diced to a pulp

1/2 medium onion, diced very fine

1/4 cup soy sauce

1 (10 ounce) can crushed pineapple

1/2 cup water

1-1/2 pounds moose steak (any cut), cut into bite size pieces

HERE'S HOW:

1. Make a sauce of the sugar, ginger, garlic, onion, soy sauce, pineapple and water.
2. Pour sauce over meat and marinate for 2 hours.
3. Spread meat pieces on shallow pan and place under a broiler or in a very hot oven, 450 degrees, for 3-5 minutes on each side.
4. Serve immediately.

Note:
This is ideal as either an hors d'oeuvre or main course.

3-4 Servings
(more as an hors d'oeuvre)

Mooseburgers

WHAT'S NEEDED:

80% moose meat

20% beef kidney suet

HERE'S HOW:

1. Combine and run through a fine grinder, twice.
2. Shape into patties.
3. Grill or pan fry.
4. Turn once, and season lightly with salt.
5. Place on a bun and eat heartily.

Moose Hash

WHAT'S NEEDED:

1/2 onion, diced fine

2 ribs celery, diced fine

1/4 cup cooking oil

1 pound potatoes, cooked, cooled, peeled and diced in 1/2" cubes

1 pound roasted moose meat, coarsely ground

1/2 teaspoon salt

1/4 teaspoon pepper

4 poached eggs

HERE'S HOW:

1. Saute the onion and celery in oil until tender. Drain.
2. Combine the onion, celery, potatoes and meat.
3. Season with salt and pepper.
4. Place in a greased casserole and bake uncovered at 350 degrees for 25-30 minutes.
5. Serve hot with poached eggs on top.

4 Servings

MOOSE MEAT BURGUNDY

WHAT'S NEEDED:

1/2 teaspoon salt

1/4 teaspoon pepper

1 cup flour

1 pound thinly sliced moose meat

1/2 pound fresh mushrooms or 1 cup canned whole
   button mushrooms

1 clove garlic, minced extra fine

1/2 cup cooking oil

1 (6 ounce) can tomato paste

3/4 cup Burgundy wine

cooked noodles or rice

HERE'S HOW:

1. Mix the salt, pepper and flour together in a bowl.
2. Dip moose in seasoned flour mixture.
3. Saute meat, mushrooms and garlic in cooking oil until brown.
4. Add tomato paste and wine.
5. Simmer covered approximately 45 minutes. Stir occasionally.
6. Serve over noodles or rice.

4 Servings

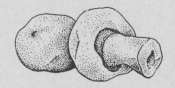

Moose Stew

WHAT'S NEEDED:

3/4 cup flour
2 teaspoons salt
1/2 teaspoon pepper
1 pound lean moose meat, cut into 1'' pieces
1/3 cup cooking oil
1/2 onion, diced
6 carrots, peeled and cut in 1'' chunks
3 ribs celery, cut in 1'' chunks
3 potatoes, peeled and cut in 1'' chunks
16 ounces canned tomato sauce
1/16 teaspoon cinnamon
water

HERE'S HOW:

1. In a paper bag mix the flour, salt and pepper.
2. Add meat, shake thoroughly until coated.
3. In a heavy skillet, prehcat oil.
4. Brown the flour coated meat and onion in oil.
5. Add remaining ingredients, covering with water.
6. Simmer, covered, approximately 1 hour.

Note:

The stew will thicken and the flavor will be magnificent.

4 Servings

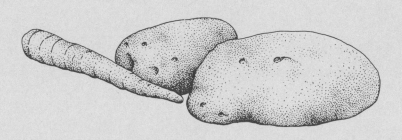

Roast Moose with Herbs

WHAT'S NEEDED:

3 Tablespoons cooking oil
1/2 teaspoon dried marjoram
1/2 teaspoon chopped basil
2 teaspoons salt
1/2 teaspoon pepper
1 clove garlic, diced very fine
1 (3 pound) moose roast

HERE'S HOW:

1. Place oil in small dish and add all spices and garlic.
2. Let stand for 30 minutes.
3. Brush roast thoroughly with oil mixture using a pastry brush.
4. Roast covered in 350 degree oven (25-30 minutes per pound). Uncover for the last 15 minutes.

4-6 Servings

Moose or Venison Sausage

WHAT'S NEEDED:

7 pounds finely ground meat (moose, venison, bear, elk)
3 pounds finely ground pork
2 Tablespoons coarse ground black pepper
2-1/2 Tablespoons salt
2 Tablespoons onion salt
2 Tablespoons garlic powder

HERE'S HOW:

1. Mix all ingredients well.
2. Form into patties.
3. Pan fry or grill.
4. Use what's needed and freeze the rest in 1 pound packages for future servings.

Moose or Venison Salami

WHAT'S NEEDED:

10 pounds finely ground meat
2 Tablespoons white pepper
1 Tablespoon ground coriander
1 Tablespoon ground ginger
1 Tablespoon ground nutmeg
2 Tablespoons ground caraway
2 Tablespoons paprika
1 Tablespoon red pepper
1/4 cup Liquid Smoke

HERE'S HOW:

1. Mix all ingredients well.
2. Roll into 3 inch (diameter) by 6 inch length rolls.
3. Bake in a 300 degree oven until a 150 degree interior temperature is reached.
4. Use what's needed and freeze the rest.

Moose or Venison Jerky

WHAT'S NEEDED:

lean game meat, cut into thin strips (partially frozen meat slices easier), approximately 1/8'' thick (1'' wide and 6-8'' in length)

garlic powder

seasoned salt

Italian seasoning

thyme

cayenne pepper

black pepper

salt

dry mustard

sage

paprika

ground allspice

HERE'S HOW:

1. Dust meat lightly with each of the above seasonings on both sides and pat in firmly by hand.
2. Place the strips on oven rack and bake for 8 hours at 150 degrees with the oven door slightly open.
3. Cool meat to room temperature.
4. Store in jars, tightly covered.

Note:
May also use caribou, elk or bear.

REINDEER

Reindeer is without a doubt the most tender of wild game meat. I have had reindeer that literally fell apart after being frozen and then thawed. The Eskimos often eat this meat raw without any cooking. This custom may or may not have derived from a lack of cooking facilities while traveling across a glacial ice pack. I have, however, sampled frozen-defrosted marinated reindeer meat. Not bad!

REINDEER STEAKS CAMP STYLE

WHAT'S NEEDED:

> reindeer steaks
> salt and pepper
> garlic powder and/or oregano
> flour
> butter or cooking oil

HERE'S HOW:

1. Season steaks on both sides with light application of salt, pepper, garlic powder and/or oregano.
2. Dredge with flour.
3. Pan fry in butter or cooking oil at fairly high heat quickly. Do not overcook.

Reindeer Roast with Oven-Browned Vegetables

WHAT'S NEEDED:

1 (4 pound) reindeer roast
2 teaspoons salt
1/2 teaspoon pepper
1 pound beef suet
1 dozen large carrots, peeled
2 ribs celery
1 clove garlic, peeled
1 large onion, peeled and halved
6 large potatoes, peeled and quartered
paprika
2 cups hot water

HERE'S HOW:

1. Season the roast with salt and pepper.
2. To prevent drying affix beef suet to top of roast with wooden picks, after it has been seasoned. Suet also provides an excellent flavor to the meat.
3. Place roast in roasting pan with carrots, celery, garlic, onion and potatoes. (Potatoes should be pre-browned slightly in a pan with deep hot grease or french fryer.)
4. Dust with paprika.
5. Bake in 350 degree oven uncovered for 45 minutes.
6. Add 2 cups hot water and continue baking until meat is tender, about 45 minutes more.

10-12 Servings

SMALL GAME

SMALL GAME

Small game is the stuff that kids come home with after a day of ''plinking.'' Small game is also the stuff the old man brings home sometimes instead of big game. He usually mumbles something about the racks not being big enough, and offers instead a three pound rabbit or squirrel as a trophy. This isn't all bad, and here are a few ways to make it better.

BEAVER AND RACCOON

While these animals "ain't" necessarily my bag, they are edible. Both critters are probably the most adaptable to baking.

BAKED BEAVER OR RACCOON

WHAT'S NEEDED:

> 1 beaver or raccoon, skinned and completely defatted
> salt and pepper
> garlic powder
> celery top from 1 rib of celery
> 1 onion, peeled
> 2 carrots, peeled
> 1/2 cup Brandy
> 2 cups water

HERE'S HOW:

1. Season the meat with salt, pepper and garlic powder.
2. Place in a roast pan with celery tops, onion and carrots.
3. Bake covered at 350 degrees for 1 hour.
4. Add the Brandy and water. Bake 1 hour and 15 minutes longer, basting occasionally with the liquid in the bottom of the pan.

16-20 Servings

Legend has it that the Fried Beaver Tail is an old trapper's delicacy. Here's a recipe from an old trapper.

FRIED BEAVER TAIL

WHAT'S NEEDED:

>   2 beaver tails
>   cold water
>   1/2 cup vinegar
>   1 Tablespoon salt
>   2 teaspoons baking soda
>   2 quarts water
>   1/2 teaspoon salt
>   1/4 teaspoon black pepper
>   1/4 cup flour
>   1/4 cup butter
>   1/2 cup dry Sherry
>   1 teaspoon medium dry mustard
>   1 teaspoon sugar
>   1/4 teaspoon garlic powder
>   1 Tablespoon Worcestershire sauce

HERE'S HOW:

1. Skin the beaver tails, clean thoroughly.
2. Let soak overnight in cold water, adding vinegar and 1 Tablespoon salt to the water.
3. Remove the tails from the brine. Rinse in cold water.
4. Add baking soda to the 2 quarts of water. Add the beaver tails. Bring to a boil. Reduce the heat and allow to simmer for 10 minutes.
5. Drain and rinse.

6. Season the beaver tails with salt and pepper and dredge in flour.
7. Saute in butter over medium heat until tender.
8. Mix the Sherry, mustard, sugar, garlic powder and Worcestershire sauce together. Add to the beaver tails and simmer very gently for about 10 minutes, basting frequently.
9. Slice and serve.

2-4 Servings

Boiled Rabbit

WHAT'S NEEDED:

1 or 2 (2-1/2 pound) rabbits, skinned and cut up
2 medium onions, peeled
2 whole carrots, peeled
4 small potatoes, peeled
salt and pepper
hot water to cover
1 teaspoon parsley flakes

HERE'S HOW:

1. Place rabbit in a cooking pot.
2. Add the onions, carrots, potatoes, salt and pepper.
3. Cover with hot water.
4. Bring to a boil, reduce heat to simmer. Cook covered for approximately 1 hour.

4-6 Servings

HASENPFEFFER

WHAT'S NEEDED:

1-1/2 cups cider vinegar
1-1/2 cups cold water
1/2 cup sugar
3 bay leaves
2 teaspoons salt
1 teaspoon whole cloves
1/4 teaspoon black pepper
1/8 teaspoon allspice
1 medium onion, sliced
3 pounds rabbit, skinned and cut up
1/2 cup flour
butter or shortening
cornstarch or arrowroot

HERE'S HOW:

1. Combine the vinegar, water, sugar, spices, seasoning and onion in a large bowl.
2. Add the cut up rabbit.
3. Cover and refrigerate for at least 12 hours, preferably a day or two.
4. Remove the rabbit and drain well. Save the marinade.
5. Dip the rabbit in flour and fry until brown in 1/4 inch of hot butter or shortening in a heavy skillet.
6. After browning, place the rabbit in a clean fry pan.
7. Add the marinade.
8. Simmer covered until the rabbit is tender, about 1 hour.

9. When the rabbit is tender, remove from the pan and thicken the remaining liquid with a paste made of small amount of cornstarch and water.

10. Serve the sauce over the rabbit.

DEEP FRIED OR OVEN BAKED RABBIT

WHAT'S NEEDED:

1 (2-1/2 pound) rabbit, skinned
salt, pepper and garlic powder
egg wash: 2 eggs and 2 Tablespoons milk, beaten together
1 cup all purpose breading (seasoned coating mix)

HERE'S HOW:

1. Split and disjoint the skinned rabbit.
2. Season with salt and pepper and garlic powder.
3. Dip in egg wash.
4. Roll in breading.
5. Deep fry for approximately 10 minutes or bake in a medium oven 350 degrees for 30 minutes.

2-3 Servings

RABBIT MULLIGATAWNY

WHAT'S NEEDED:

2 (2-1/2 pound) rabbits, skinned, quartered and deboned
1/4 cup butter
2 cups cooked rice
1 pint of Basic Cream Sauce (see index)
1/2 teaspoon salt
1/4 teaspoon black pepper
1 teaspoon paprika
1 teaspoon curry powder
6 strips crisp bacon, crumbled
1 green apple, split in half, cored and diced to 1/4'' chunks

HERE'S HOW:

1. Saute the rabbits in butter until they are brown.
2. Mix remaining ingredients and place with rabbit in a large covered casserole or baking dish and bake at 325 degrees for 25 minutes.

4-6 Servings

Rabbit Lorenzo

WHAT'S NEEDED:

2 (2-1/2 pound) rabbits, skinned, deboned and cut in 1" chunks

1/2 cup butter

1/2 medium onion, diced fine

1 medium green pepper, diced fine

1 (4 ounce) can mushroom caps

2 whole canned pimentos, diced coarsely

1/2 teaspoon salt

1/4 teaspoon pepper

1 teaspoon medium dry mustard

2 ounces dry white wine

1 pint of Cream Sauce (see index)

HERE'S HOW:

1. Saute the rabbit in 1/4 cup butter in a heavy fry pan until browned.
2. In a separate pan, saute the onion, green pepper and mushroom caps until they are translucent or *very* lightly browned.
3. Drain the butter from the rabbit and vegetables and transfer both to a casserole or baking dish.
4. Add remaining ingredients.
5. Mix well. Cover and bake in a 325 degree oven for 25-30 minutes.

4-6 Servings

PAN FRIED SQUIRREL

WHAT'S NEEDED:

> 1 squirrel, skinned, cleaned and disjointed
> salt and pepper
> onion salt
> egg wash: 1 egg, 1 Tablespoon milk, beaten together
> 1/2 cup flour
> butter for frying
> 1/4 ounce Brandy

HERE'S HOW:

1. Season the squirrel with salt, pepper and onion salt.
2. Dip in egg wash.
3. Dip in flour.

4. Fry in deep hot butter in a thick fry pan to which the Brandy has been added.

5. Since the pieces are very small and should not be overcooked, watch them closely. When they are brown, they are done.

2 Servings

SQUIRREL IN ALMOND SAUCE

WHAT'S NEEDED:

3 or 4 squirrels, skinned and disjointed
butter
1 pint of Basic Cream Sauce (see index)
3/4 cup almonds, slivered or sliced
1/2 teaspoon almond paste or 2-3 drops almond extract
salt and pepper
yellow food coloring
Baking Powder Biscuits (see index)

HERE'S HOW:

1. Saute the squirrels in butter in a heavy fry pan until golden brown.

2. Add the Cream Sauce to cover the squirrels.

3. Add the almonds, almond paste or extract and salt and pepper.

4. A few drops of yellow food coloring will improve the appearance.

5. Simmer covered for 30-40 minutes.

6. Serve with Baking Powder Biscuits.

4-6 Servings

SAUTEED SQUIRREL IN BURGUNDY SAUCE

WHAT'S NEEDED:

> 2 or 3 squirrels, skinned, cleaned and disjointed
> butter
> 1/4 onion, peeled and diced
> 1 teaspoon parsley flakes
> 1 bay leaf
> dash of thyme
> dash of ground cloves
> dash of mace
> 1 pint Beef Stock (see index)
> 1 cup Burgundy wine
> cornstarch or arrowroot and water

HERE'S HOW:

1. Saute the squirrel in butter in a heavy fry pan until golden brown.
2. Drain the butter from the pan.
3. Add the onion, spices, Beef Stock and wine.
4. Thicken the sauce very slightly with a paste made of cornstarch or arrowroot and water.
5. Simmer covered on low heat for approximately 30 minutes.

4-6 Servings

CURRIED SQUIRREL

WHAT'S NEEDED:

    2 or 3 disjointed squirrels
    2 Tablespoons butter
    1/2 medium onion, diced very fine
    1/4 cup dry Sherry
    1 pint Basic Cream Sauce (see index)
    1/2 teaspoon curry powder
    salt and pepper
    yellow food coloring
    1 cup rice, boiled

HERE'S HOW:

1. Saute the squirrel in butter in a heavy fry pan.
2. Remove the squirrel from fry pan and saute the onion until translucent.
3. Add the Sherry, Cream Sauce, curry powder and squirrel.
4. Season lightly with salt and pepper.
5. Add a drop or two of food coloring.
6. Simmer covered for 30 minutes.
7. Serve over boiled white rice.

4-6 Servings

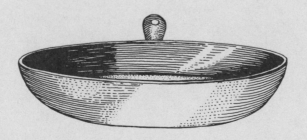

SNAPPING TURTLE

I don't know if this "lowly beast" can be considered game or not, but once one gets by the shell, the meat within is excellent. The snapping turtle can attain very large size. Once while fishing with my young sons, we had a fairly decent catch of bass and northern on our stringer when a turtle spotted them and decided they would be a very good lunch. We managed to push him away with an oar and save our catch, but I swear that turtle weighed 200 pounds and was three feet in diameter. What a great stew he would have made.

BAKED TURTLE

WHAT'S NEEDED:

> 2-3 pounds turtle meat, cut into 1-1/2" chunks
> salt and pepper
> egg wash: 2 eggs, 2 Tablespoons milk, beaten together
> 1 cup all purpose breading (seasoned coating mix)
> 3/4 cup cooking oil

HERE'S HOW:

1. Season turtle meat with salt and pepper.
2. Dip in egg wash.
3. Roll in breading.
4. Heat cooking oil in heavy fry pan, add breaded turtle meat and brown slightly.
5. Place on a baking sheet and bake at 350 degrees for about 45 minutes.

4-6 Servings

FRIED TURTLE

WHAT'S NEEDED:

2 pounds turtle meat, cut into 3/4″ chunks
salt and pepper
3/4 cup flour
1/2 cup butter
6 ounces drained, canned mushroom caps
1/2 onion, diced medium
1 clove garlic, diced to a pulp
1 green pepper, cut into 1″ chunks
1 (8 ounce) can tomato sauce
1/2 cup white wine
1/2 cup water
cayenne pepper
2 beef bouillon cubes
White or Wild Rice (see index)

HERE'S HOW:

1. Season turtle meat with salt and pepper.
2. Put flour in paper bag, add turtle meat a few pieces at a time and shake until completely coated with flour.
3. Heat butter in a heavy fry pan, add turtle meat, mushrooms, onion, garlic and green pepper and fry until golden brown.
4. Add tomato sauce, white wine, water, dash of cayenne and beef bouillon cubes.
5. Simmer, covered for approximately 1 hour.
6. Serve with either white or wild rice.

4-6 Servings

TURTLE STEW

3 or 4 pounds of turtle meat, cut into 1" chunks
salt and pepper
3/4 cup flour
1/2 cup cooking oil
1 large onion, diced coarse
6 large potatoes, peeled, cut into 1-1/2" chunks
6-8 carrots, cleaned and cut into 1-1/2" chunks
8 ribs celery, cut into 1" chunks
3 (8 ounce) cans tomato sauce
3 teaspoons granulated beef bouillon or base
hot water

HERE'S HOW:

1. Season the cut up turtle meat with salt and pepper.
2. Put the flour into a paper bag, add the turtle meat a few pieces at a time and shake until the meat is evenly coated with flour.
3. Heat the cooking oil in a heavy fry pan, add meat and fry until it is browned.
4. Transfer the browned meat and remaining ingredients to a large kettle or pot.
5. Add enough hot water to barely cover.
6. Simmer covered at low heat for approximately 1 hour, or until the vegetables are completely cooked.

6-8 Servings

EXOTICS

THE EXOTICS

A lot of fun and many fine parties can be had with all kinds of wild game, but nothing seems to grab people like the so-called exotic game animals such as: elephant, lion, tiger, hippo, llama, camel and so forth. I once listed Roast Sirloin of Elephant as a noon special on my menu. The reaction was absolutely beautiful to behold. If there were two or more people in a party, be assured that one person ordered it and that all would sample it. I think their greatest surprise was that it tasted good.

I have never hunted African game, although if the good Lord is willing, I would like to take a whack at it someday. I do know, however, that while taste and texture may vary somewhat and while certain spices and seasonings will tend to accentuate or control the flavor of some meats, you need not be afraid, it isn't bad tasting. I am going to show you a few forms of preparation for a few exotic animals that we have prepared for various parties. This will certainly not be a listing of every species of every animal that roams the earth, but rather a few that I have had direct experience with and have found to be most palatable.

You have no doubt seen the all time classic recipe for the preparation of elephant, however, you're about to get it again.

ELEPHANT

WHAT'S NEEDED:

> 1 elephant
> salt and pepper
> 2 rabbits

HERE'S HOW:

1. Cut elephant into bite size pieces. (This usually takes 2 months).
2. Add enough gravy to cover, about 400 gallons.
3. Cook over kerosene stove for about 5 weeks at 450 degrees.
4. This will serve about 3000 people. If more show up for dinner, add the rabbits. However, you have to be careful as most people don't like hare in their food.

3000 Servings

African Lion or Tiger

The big cats have an absolutely unique and distinctive flavor. In texture and appearance they are much like pork. The loins of lion or tiger may be handled much the same as loin of llama, with the possible exception that a bit of ground rosemary might be substituted for the oregano. I feel that the meat should be at least cooked to medium-well or well-done.

Roast Round of African Lion or Tiger

WHAT'S NEEDED:

> 1 (4 pound) roast of lion or tiger
> 2 Tablespoons salt
> 2 Tablespoons black pepper
> 1/2 Tablespoon rosemary
> 2 cloves garlic, peeled
> 1/2 small onion, peeled
> 2 ribs celery
> 1/2 pound beef suet
> 1 pint hot water
> 2 ounces Cognac
> Bordelaise Sauce (see index)

HERE'S HOW:

1. Place the roast in a baking pan.
2. Season with salt, pepper and rosemary.
3. Add garlic, onion and celery to the pan.
4. Spike on the beef suet with wooden picks.
5. Bake in a moderate 350 degree oven for 1 hour.
6. Add 1 pint hot water and Cognac.
7. Return to oven for 1 hour, basting frequently with the liquid in the pan.
8. Serve with Bordelaise Sauce.

Note:

These are very dry meats, overcooking will make them tough.

6-8 Servings

CAMEL

The good folks of the East long ago discovered that the camel and curry powder seemed to have an affinity for one another. Here's a quick little method for astounding your bridge club or poker party.

CURRIED CAMEL MULLIGATAWNY

WHAT'S NEEDED:

butter or cooking oil

1 pound camel meat, cut in 1/2'' cubes (we've tried the hind leg but have been informed that the hump meat, because of its fatty content, is preferable.)

1 whole green onion, diced

1/2 clove garlic, diced to a pulp

2 ribs celery, cut into 1/2'' chunks

3 cups cooked white rice

1/2 teaspoon salt

1/2 teaspoon coarsely ground pepper

1/2 teaspoon MSG or Accent (optional)

1 green apple, cored and diced into 1/2'' cubes

curry powder, to taste

2 or 3 cups (as needed) of Basic Cream Sauce (see index)

paprika

HERE'S HOW:

1. In a sauce pan, with butter or cooking oil, saute the diced camel meat at medium heat until it is completely cooked.

2. In a separate pan, saute the onion, garlic and celery in butter or cooking oil until tender.
3. Mix camel meat, vegetables and cooked rice together.
4. Season with salt, pepper, MSG or Accent (optional).
5. Add diced apple.
6. Season to taste with curry powder.
7. Add 2 cups Cream Sauce.
8. Place in a baking dish, dust with paprika.
9. Bake in 400 degree oven for 40 minutes.

4-6 Servings

ELAND

The eland is one of Africa's most sought after trophies. It is of the antelope family and the meat is excellent.

BAKED ELAND BORDELAISE

WHAT'S NEEDED:

1 (3 pound) eland round
cooking oil
salt and pepper

HERE'S HOW:

1. Brush eland with cooking oil.
2. Salt and pepper to taste.
3. Bake on a flat tray at 350 degrees for about 60 minutes or until medium rare.
4. Remove from oven. Slice thinly, about 1/4 inch.
5. Serve very hot with Bordelaise Sauce (see index).

6-8 Servings

ELEPHANT TRUNK

I once ordered an elephant trunk for a party and received a piece of meat approximately 100 pounds in weight, taken from the upper trunk region of the animal. It was coarse in texture, rather bland with no distinctive flavor, yet surprisingly tender. We roasted this in three equal pieces. This meat did not have a great deal of fat and we prepared it very much as any other roast of domestic meat. So should you come into possession of a piece of elephant trunk, prepare it as follows.

ELEPHANT TRUNK ROAST

WHAT'S NEEDED:

> 1 (5 pound) elephant trunk piece
> 1/4 cup salt
> 2 cloves garlic
> 1/2 teaspoon black pepper
> 3 ribs celery, tops included
> 1/2 onion, peeled
> 1/2 pound beef suet

HERE'S HOW:

1. Season with spices as listed.
2. Affix the suet to the meat, using picks to hold it in place.
3. Bake in long pan, covered, at 325 degrees for 2 hours 30 minutes.

Note:
This can be served with Brown Gravy or a Bordelaise Sauce (see index).

10-12 Servings

LOIN OF LLAMA

WHAT'S NEEDED:

1 (7-9 pound) loin of llama
1/4 cup salt
1 teaspoon coarse black pepper
1/2 teaspoon oregano
2 cloves garlic, cut into 1/16" strips
paprika

HERE'S HOW:

1. Remove any fat from the roast.
2. Season with the above spices, puncturing holes approximately 2 inches apart the length of the loin and insert about a dozen spikes of garlic.
3. Dust with paprika.
4. Roast at 350 degrees for approximately 1½ hour.

Note:

Do not overcook this meat as it will dry out and become very tough.

18-20 Servings

Breaded Llama Chops

WHAT'S NEEDED:

> 4 llama chops, cut 1'' thick
> salt and pepper
> garlic powder
> oregano
> egg wash: 2 eggs, 2 Tablespoons milk, beaten together
> your favorite breading
> butter or cooking oil

HERE'S HOW:

1. Season llama chop to taste with salt, pepper, garlic powder and oregano.
2. Dip in egg wash, then in breading.
3. Cook in butter or cooking oil at medium heat, for approximately 5 minutes per side or until medium done.

4 Servings

Broiled Llama Chops

WHAT'S NEEDED:

4 llama chops, cut 1'' thick
cooking oil
salt and pepper
garlic powder
oregano
1/8 cup fresh lemon juice

HERE'S HOW:

1. Brush chops with cooking oil.
2. Season to taste with salt, pepper and just a touch of garlic powder.
3. Add a light sprinkling of oregano.
4. Broil approximately 5 minutes per side. Do not overcook, these should be medium.
5. Remove from broiler and add a couple drops of fresh lemon juice.

4 Servings

HIPPOPOTAMUS

I have mixed emotions regarding these huge beasts. They can be good or bad, gastronomically speaking. When they are good, they are edible, when they are bad, they aren't. They can be cut into steaks and pan fried or grilled. They can be diced or cut into cubes and stewed. Or the meat can be roasted. The meat has no distinctive flavor and is inclined to be tough, but at least you could say that you had eaten hippo. Without going into a great deal of detail, I would recommend that you handle this exactly as you would your favorite beef dish.

HIPPO STEAKS

WHAT'S NEEDED:

> 4 hippo steaks, cut approximately 1/2'' thick
> salt and pepper
> egg wash: 2 eggs, 2 Tablespoons milk, beaten together
> flour, as needed
> butter or cooking oil
> Brown Gravy (see index)
> Sherry

HERE'S HOW:

1. Season steaks with salt and pepper.
2. Dip in egg wash, then in flour.
3. Pan fry, covered, in hot butter or cooking oil until medium well, approximately 4-5 minutes per side.
4. Serve with Brown Gravy to which a dash of Sherry has been added. Just a dash, no more.

4 Servings

OSTRICH

The original ''Big Bird''! At 300 or more pounds it's more than big, it's huge. Here are a couple of methods of reducing it to bite size.

OSTRICH SALAD OR SANDWICH

WHAT'S NEEDED:

> 1/2 pound ground ostrich meat, cooked and cooled
> 5 cups diced celery
> 1 whole pimento, diced
> 2 cups mayonnaise
> salt and pepper to taste
> 1/4 teaspoon poultry seasoning
> 1/2 teaspoon MSG (optional)

HERE'S HOW:

1. Mix all ingredients well.
2. Serve on lettuce leaves with sliced tomatoes as a salad or on pumpernickle bread as a sandwich.

6-8 Servings

OSTRICH STEAK

WHAT'S NEEDED:

> salt and pepper
>
> 4 slices ostrich meat, cut about 1/4 inch thick and 6 inches in length (you may want a butcher to slice it for you)
>
> egg wash: 2 eggs, 2 Tablespoons milk, beaten together
>
> cracker meal
>
> cooking oil or butter

HERE'S HOW:

1. Salt and pepper meat to taste.
2. Dip in egg wash and then in cracker meal.
3. Grill or pan fry in cooking oil or butter.

4 Servings

FISH

FISH

Fish demand immediate attention in warm weather. The gills will begin to deteriorate as soon as they die. Fish should be dressed as soon as possible. With a sharp knife, remove the entire head and gill structure. Make an incision the length of the body, along the belly of the fish and remove the intestines. Rinse thoroughly. Remove scales or filet and skin the fish.

Ron Schara has long enjoyed a reputation as an outstanding writer, author, hunter, fisherman, bon vivant and trencherman par excellence. Some of my fish recipes appear in Ron Schara's excellent and definitive ''Minnesota Fishing Guide,'' and have been helpful to those who have enjoyed this marvelous book.

Fish recipes remain the same regardless of the type of fish used. The great northern, walleye, lake trout, Arctic char and salmon all respond well to similar cooking methods. Fresh water fish, because of their delicate flavor and naturally moist texture, should never be overcooked. The instant that the flesh loses its translucent appearance, it is done and should be removed from any further exposure to heat.

Walleyes provide the finest eating of all fresh water fish. I prefer a freshly caught, skinned filet of walleye, lightly seasoned with salt and pepper, dipped in egg wash and breading and deep fried, to any other fish around.

THE SHORE DINNER

The shore dinner lends itself to the vagaries of mosqui-
toes, dust, and wind and misplaced tsetse flies. Maybe
I'm getting old. I used to enjoy this sort of thing but I see
it now as an abomination, a necessary evil forced upon
one by circumstance, poor planning or the self inflicted
discomforts perpetrated in the guise of fun or pleasure or
sport. Anyhow, if you're caught out, here's what you
can do about it: Have a generous supply of bug repellent,
matches, aluminum foil and get with it. Seriously, the
shore dinner can be a tasty and rewarding experience.
There is really nothing better to eat than freshly caught
fish.

NOTE: If you are in the mood for an elegant shore
dinner, gather up your friends and fly in lobster and have
a New England lobster feed. The more people involved,
the less cost you will have to pay for airfare of your
lobster.
1. Boil lobsters in large pots.
2. Fresh corn on the cob is easy to cook.
3. Boil potatoes in water.
Remember butter to put on all three and enjoy. To
heighten your dinner — serve champagne!

OUTDOOR AMANDINE

WHAT'S NEEDED:

- fish, freshly caught
- salt and pepper
- paprika (not necessary, but a nice touch)
- slivered almonds
- butter
- fresh lemon juice
- 1 raw washed potato per person
- 1 ear of corn (fresh or frozen) per person
- aluminum foil
- a loaf of bread
- a jug of wine or beer or anything else with alcohol in it to ward off tsetse fly or other vermin

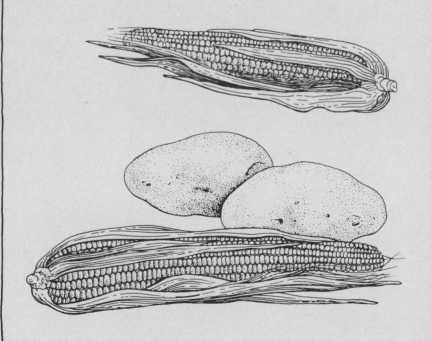

HERE'S HOW:

1. Catch a fish, any fish.
2. Fillet and skin the fillets.
3. Season with salt and pepper and add a dash of paprika. Sprinkle with almonds, add a few chunks of butter and a few drops of lemon juice.
4. Wrap in foil, sealing well.
5. Wrap a potato in foil.
6. Wrap an ear of corn in foil, adding a little butter and salt.
7. Build a fire and reduce it to coals. (A little charcoal is advisable if it isn't too cumbersome to carry around).
8. Bake in this order:
   First, the potato for 30 minutes.
   Next, throw the corn in the fire for 20 minutes.
   Then lay the fish on the hot coals. (A wire rack of some sort is advisable.) When the fish has cooked for approximately 10 minutes, turn it and cook for another 5-7 minutes. The corn and potatoes should, of course, be turned frequently while baking. With a little luck, everything should be done about the same time.
9. Eat, drink and be merry!

ARCTIC CHAR

Arctic char is the "King of North American Game Fish". It is found only in the icy waters of the far North. The char is not a huge fish. The world record is about 28 pounds, although Eskimos and Indians tell of netting char that weighed 60 to 80 pounds. The delicate flavor of this fish is recognized by gourmets world wide. In texture and flavor it is somewhat between salmon and Arctic lake trout. The flesh of this fish is prized to the extent that char is still used as a medium of exchange in many areas of the far North.

GRILLED OR PAN FRIED ARCTIC CHAR

WHAT'S NEEDED:

>	2 eggs
>	2 Tablespoons milk
>	4 (8 ounce) char fillets
>	salt and pepper
>	3/4 cup flour
>	1/4 cup butter
>	1 lemon, cut in wedges

HERE'S HOW:

1. Place eggs and milk in a flat pan or dish. Mix well.
2. Season fillets to taste with salt and pepper.
3. Dip fillets into egg mixture and dredge in flour.
4. Fry over medium heat in butter, turn once and cook until done. CAUTION: Do not overcook (5-6 minutes).
5. Serve with lemon wedges.

4 Servings

BAKED CHAR NEWBURG

WHAT'S NEEDED:

- 1/2 teaspoon black pepper
- 1/2 teaspoon salt
- 1/2 cup flour
- 3 (8 ounce) char fillets
- 1/4 cup butter
- 2 hard boiled eggs, diced coarsely
- 4 ounces whole button mushrooms, sauteed in butter until brown
- 3 ounces dry Sherry
- 1 pint Basic Cream Sauce (see index)
- dash of paprika

HERE'S HOW:

1. Mix the salt, pepper and flour.
2. Dip the fillets in the seasoned flour.
3. Pan fry or grill in butter until slightly browned on both sides.
4. Place the fillets in a casserole or a baking pan.
5. Add the egg, mushrooms and Sherry to the Cream Sauce and mix carefully.
6. Pour the sauce over the fish, dust with paprika and bake covered in a 350 degree oven for 20-25 minutes.

3 Servings

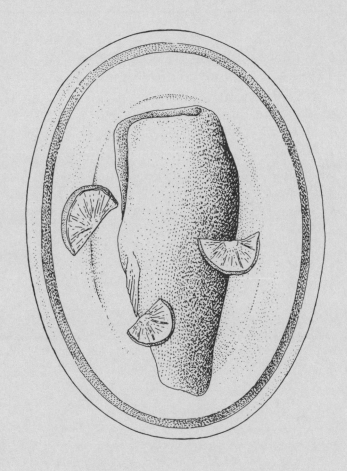

Whole Baked Arctic Char

WHAT'S NEEDED:

> 1 large char, cleaned
> 1/2 pound butter, softened
> salt and pepper
> 1 lemon (use 1/2 for juice, 1/2 for wedges)

HERE'S HOW:

1. Wash char thoroughly in cold water.
2. Place 1/4 pound butter in body cavity and season with salt and pepper.
3. Seal in foil, place in baking pan.
4. Bake in hot oven at 375 degrees for about 20 minutes.
5. Remove from oven and add other 1/4 pound butter to char. Squeeze juice of 1/2 lemon on fish. Reseal in foil and return to oven for 30 minutes.
6. Serve with lemon wedges.

2 Servings

Broiled Char with Hollandaise Sauce

WHAT'S NEEDED:

2 (8 ounce) char fillets
1/4 cup melted butter
salt and pepper
paprika
Hollandaise Sauce (see index)

HERE'S HOW:

1. Brush fillets with butter.
2. Season with salt and pepper. Dust with paprika.
3. Place under broiler for 3 minutes on each side.
4. Serve topped with Hollandaise Sauce.

2 Servings

Baked Stuffed Char

WHAT'S NEEDED:

1 (3 pound) char or 3 pound section of larger fish (leave whole, head may be removed if desired)
salt and pepper
Basic Stuffing (see index), sufficient to stuff cavity of fish
3 Tablespoons melted butter
1 teaspoon parsley flakes
1/4 lemon, juiced

HERE'S HOW:

1. Wash fish thoroughly with cold water.
2. Season body cavity with salt and pepper. Stuff with Basic Stuffing.
3. Place cavity side down on sheet of foil. Pour melted butter over fish and sprinkle with parsley flakes.
4. Squeeze lemon juice over fish.
5. Seal the foil to form a bag.
6. Place the fish on a baking sheet and bake at 350 degrees for about 45 minutes.

Note:

Baked stuffed char is excellent wrapped in Wellington Pastry (see index). Use steps 1-4 if pastry is used.

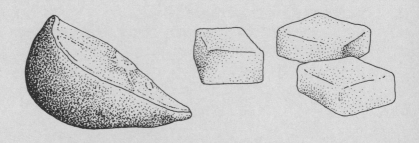

DOLPHIN

This is a common dolphin, not a porpoise (Hawaiian Walleye of sorts). It is one of the better game fish and may be treated as we have treated shark. The usual caution applies. Don't overcook!

MAHI MAHI

WHAT'S NEEDED:

> 1 cup white rice
> 3 cups salted water
> 1 clove garlic, diced to a pulp
> 2 green onions, diced fine
> butter
> salt and pepper
> 3/4 ounce Cognac
> 1/2 ounce Pernod
> fillet of ocean fish

HERE'S HOW:

1. In a sauce pan cover the rice with lightly salted water, bring to a boil, covered, allowing it to cook until the rice is approximately 3/4 done, about 30 minutes.
2. In a separate skillet, saute the garlic and onion in butter until golden brown and mix with rice.
3. Season to taste with salt and pepper.
4. Add Cognac and Pernod.
5. Place the fillet on top of the rice.
6. Cover tightly and simmer, until rice is tender and fish is steamed.

3-4 Servings

FROG

Here we are talking about the giant Bullfrog of Louisiana fame, not the little green frog that should be used as bass bait.

FROG LEGS

WHAT'S NEEDED:

> 8 frog legs, skinned by removing the lower leg and foot section at the 2nd joint
>
> salt and pepper
>
> garlic powder
>
> egg wash: 2 eggs, 2 Tablespoons milk, beaten together
>
> 1 cup all purpose breading (seasoned coating mix)
>
> butter or cooking oil
>
> Maitre d'Hotel Sauce (see index)

HERE'S HOW:

1. Season frog legs with salt, pepper and garlic powder.
2. Dip in egg wash and roll in breading.
3. French fry or pan fry in deep butter or cooking oil until golden brown.
4. Serve with Maitre d'Hotel Sauce.

4 Servings

FRIED LOBSTER

WHAT'S NEEDED:

> lobster meat
> butter
> 1/2 ounce Cognac
> coarse ground pepper
> paprika

HERE'S HOW:

1. Remove lobster meat from the shell and cut into 1 inch chunks.
2. Melt butter to 1/4 inch deep in skillet.
3. Add lobster and Cognac to heated butter.
4. Season lightly with pepper.
5. Dust with paprika.
6. Simmer, covered, turning lobster occasional'
   until it is cooked, about 5-6 minutes.

Note:
Don't Overcook!

FRIED SCALLOPS

These little gems can be handled as in the recipe for Fried Lobster. Add a dash of oregano and break out the cold beer!

PICKLED NORTHERN

Somewhere along the way most everyone takes a shot at pickling fish. I've tried a number of pickled fish recipes and this is the best I have found. Pickled fish makes a fine appetizer before any dinner, game or otherwise. It will keep almost indefinitely when refrigerated and serves nicely with crackers, cheese and various beverages as a snack.

DR. SATHER'S PICKLED NORTHERNS

WHAT'S NEEDED:

> Skinned northern fillets, cut into herring size (about 1-1/2 inches)

HERE'S HOW:

1. Soak in brine solution consisting of:
   4 cups water
   1 cup coarse salt
   Use plastic or glass containers, one gallon size. Do not pack (about 2/3 full of fish is enough).
2. Soak in brine for 4 days (KEEP REFRIGERATED) before putting in pickling solution.

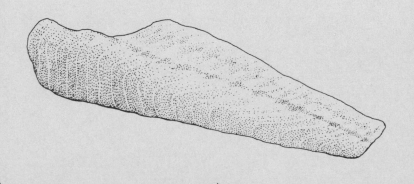

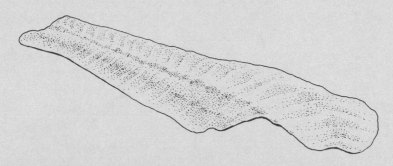

Pickling Solution

WHAT'S NEEDED:

2 cups white vinegar
5 medium white onions, sliced
5 lemons, sliced
2 teaspoons mustard seed
1-3/4 cups sugar
4 bay leaves
5 whole cloves
1 teaspoon whole allspice
1 teaspoon whole black peppercorns
5-6 red peppers
few drops Tabasco

HERE'S HOW:

1. Mix all ingredients together and bring pickling solution to a boil, then cool.
2. Remove fish from brine solution and place in clean gallon container.
3. Add pickling solution to cover fish. If more solution is needed, add white wine (Rhine or Sauterne).
4. Cover and refrigerate a minimum of 1 week before using (2-3 weeks is much better).

Here's a recipe that can be used with any good sized fish, something in the 5 pound and up class. I have titled this as Baked Northern, but believe me, any fresh fish stuffed and baked is really magnificent. I still feel, after many years of frying, baking, broiling and other assorted methods of preparation, that the simple stuffing and baking of fish is hard to beat for family style dining.

BAKED NORTHERN

WHAT'S NEEDED:

northern pike or any good sized fish

HERE'S HOW:

1. Clean and scale fish. Remove head and fins (a "V" shaped notch cut at each side of fins will remove bones).
2. Rinse thoroughly in cold water, stuff fish cavity with stuffing of your choice and place cavity side down in a well greased pan.
3. Pour sauce over fish, cover with foil tent and bake until fork may be easily inserted in flesh. (15-20 minutes per pound at 350 degrees.)

Note:
See index for Stuffings and Sauces.

4-6 Servings

Mako Shark

It seems to come as a surprise to many people that shark is edible. It is! Shark is an excellent game fish.

Baked Shark

WHAT'S NEEDED:

>2 pounds shark fillet, cut into 4-6'' pieces
>butter
>1/2 cup mushroom caps, fresh or canned
>2 cups Basic Cream Sauce (see index)
>salt
>white pepper
>2 ounces dry white wine
>paprika

HERE'S HOW:

1. Saute shark in butter until golden brown.
2. Remove fillets and place in a baking dish.
3. Saute mushrooms in butter until slightly browned and transfer to baking dish.
4. Season Cream Sauce with salt and pepper to taste.
5. Add white wine to sauce and stir.
6. Pour enough sauce over the fish to cover it. Sprinkle with paprika.
7. Bake covered in a 350 degree oven for approximately 30 minutes.

4-6 Servings

BROILED SHARK

WHAT'S NEEDED:

fillets to be broiled, 1/2 pound per person
salt and pepper
paprika
Maitre d'Hotel Sauce (see index)
fresh lemon slices

HERE'S HOW:

1. Season fillets with salt and pepper.
2. Dust with paprika.
3. Place under broiler for 5-6 minutes each side, depending on the thickness of the fillet.
4. Serve with Maitre d'Hotel Sauce and lemon slices for garnish.

PAN FRIED SHARK

WHAT'S NEEDED:

shark fillets, 1/2 pound per person
salt and pepper
cornstarch or arrowroot
Beer Batter (see index)
butter

WHAT'S NEEDED:

1. Season fillets with salt and pepper to taste.
2. Dredge with cornstarch.
3. Dip in Beer Batter.
4. Pan fry in butter, turning once.

GRAYLING

The grayling is the Arctic sailfish. Its high dorsal fin and fighting prowess make it a prized trophy for fly fishermen of the Arctic. A member of the trout family, this fish has supplied many fishermen with a tasty shore dinner.

PAN FRIED ARCTIC GRAYLING

WHAT'S NEEDED:

> 1 grayling per person
> egg wash: 1 egg and 1 Tablespoon milk
> 1/2 cup flour, or cornmeal, or cracker crumbs
> 1/2 teaspoon salt
> 1/4 teaspoon pepper
> 4 Tablespoons butter or cooking oil

HERE'S HOW:

1. Clean and wash fish.
2. Beat egg and milk together thoroughly.
3. Mix flour, salt and pepper. Dip fish in egg wash.
4. Dredge in flour or other coating.
5. Fry in butter or cooking oil. Turn once.

1 Serving

TROUT

Trout from the lakes of "Southern" Canada (Southern being below the Northwest Territories), have a tendency to be a bit stronger in flavor and somewhat richer in oils than those taken from the icy waters of the more Northern lakes. I suppose it is the same fish, but it does seem to make a difference where the lake trout is caught. Generally, the larger trout, those in the 8 pound and up class, are better baked than fried or broiled.

BAKED STUFFED BROOK OR RAINBOW TROUT

WHAT'S NEEDED:

> 1/2 pound of diced canned or frozen crab meat
> 1/2 pound of finely diced cooked shrimp
> 2 egg yolks
> 1/2 teaspoon cornstarch
> salt and pepper
> 1 Tablespoon of diced pimento
> juice of 1/2 lemon
> 4 (8-12 ounce) trout
> Hollandaise Sauce (see index)

HERE'S HOW:

1. Mix together all stuffing ingredients.
2. Salt and pepper to taste.
3. Stuff the trout with stuffing mixture.
4. Bake in a moderate 350 degree oven for 30 minutes or until fish is done.
5. Remove from oven and top with Hollandaise Sauce.

4 Servings

FILLET OF LAKE TROUT WITH BERCY BUTTER

WHAT'S NEEDED:

1/2 cup soft butter
2 Tablespoons white wine
1/2 clove garlic, minced extremely fine
1 green onion, diced very fine
dash cayenne
4 (8 ounce) trout fillets
4 Tablespoons melted butter
salt and pepper
paprika

HERE'S HOW:

1. To the 1/2 cup soft butter, add white wine, garlic, green onion and cayenne. Mix thoroughly to form Bercy Butter.
2. Let stand for 15 minutes before using. (This butter may be refrigerated and stored for an extended period of time.)
3. Brush fillets with melted plain butter.
4. Season with salt and pepper. Dust with paprika.
5. Place under broiler, turn once. Cook until done.
6. Remove from heat and top with Bercy Butter.

4 Servings

BROOK TROUT MEUNIERE

WHAT'S NEEDED:

> 4 trout or any other panfish
> 3/4 cup milk
> 1/4 teaspoon salt
> 1/4 teaspoon coarse pepper
> 2 cups flour
> butter for sauteing
> Meuniere Sauce (see index)

HERE'S HOW:

1. Dress and wash trout. Dip in milk to which salt and coarse pepper have been added, then dip in flour.
2. Saute in butter until browned on both sides.
3. If fish are small, they may be completely cooked in this manner. If large, place in well greased pan and completely cook in a moderate 325 degree oven until they are done.
4. Serve with Meuniere Sauce.

4 Servings

LAKE TROUT BAKED WITH HERBS

WHAT'S NEEDED:

> 1 (8 ounce) trout fillet per person
> 4 Tablespoons melted butter
> salt and pepper
> basil
> thyme
> 1 lemon, sliced thin
> 1 orange, sliced thin
> paprika

HERE'S HOW:

1. Place fillets on baking sheet. Brush with melted butter.
2. Season to taste with salt, pepper, basil and thyme.
3. Alternate lemon and orange slices on top of fillet.
4. Dust with paprika.
5. Bake at 375 degrees for about 15 minutes.

BAKED WHITEFISH IN ALMOND SAUCE

WHAT'S NEEDED:

1 (2-3 pound) whitefish, scaled; head, tail and fins removed

4 Tablespoons butter

1-1/2 pints Basic Cream Sauce (see index)

1/2 teaspoon almond paste or 1/4 teaspoon almond extract

2 ounces slivered almonds

yellow food coloring

paprika

HERE'S HOW:

1. In a large heavy pan, brown fish in the butter.
2. Place in a deep baking dish.
3. Mix the Basic Cream Sauce with paste or extract and slivered almonds, add a few drops of yellow food coloring. Mix well.
4. Cover the fish with sauce.
5. Bake covered at 350 degrees for about one hour, remove and dust with paprika.

3-4 Servings

POACHED WHITEFISH OR
POOR MAN'S LOBSTER

WHAT'S NEEDED:

- 1 small bunch celery tops
- 1/4 small onion, peeled
- 1 bay leaf
- 1 quart water
- 1/2 teaspoon salt
- 1 (2-3 pound) whitefish, scaled, head, tail and fins removed, cut into 2'' chunks
- parsley flakes
- 1 lemon, cut in wedges
- 1/2 cup butter, melted

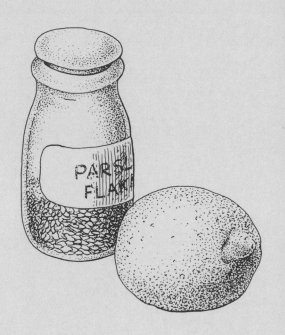

HERE'S HOW:

1. Tie the celery, onion, and bay leaf in a cheese cloth bag. Immerse in boiling water and simmer for 5 minutes.
2. Add salt to water, add the fish. Simmer covered for 10 minutes or until done.
3. Remove from water, drain.
4. Sprinkle with parsley flakes.
5. Serve with lemon wedges and butter.

3-4 Servings

Collins Beer Batter Fish

WHAT'S NEEDED:

2 eggs, beaten
12 ounces beer
1-1/2 cups flour
1/4 teaspoon salt
1/4 teaspoon pepper
1/4 teaspoon nutmeg
1/2 teaspoon baking powder
milk, if needed
6 fish fillets
cornstarch (for dredging)
Tartar Sauce (see index)

HERE'S HOW:

1. Combine beaten eggs and beer.
2. Add dry ingredients all at once. Mix until smooth, adjust consistency as required. (Moisture content of flour may vary. If batter is heavy, adjust with a small amount of milk. If batter is too thin, adjust with cornstarch.) DO NOT OVERMIX.
3. Dredge fish lightly in cornstarch.
4. Shake off excess, dip fish in batter and immerse directly into deep fat.
5. Fry at about 375 degrees until golden brown.
6. Serve immediately with Tartar Sauce.

6 Servings

COLLINS BREADED FISH FILLETS

WHAT'S NEEDED:

2 eggs

1/4 cup milk

salt and pepper

fish fillets (lake trout, walleye, northern pike, char, crappies, sunfish, etc.)

all purpose breading (seasoned coating mix)

cooking oil

1/2 cup melted butter

1/2 lemon, cut in wedges

HERE'S HOW:

1. Whip the eggs lightly in a flat pan.
2. Add milk and mix gently. Season the fillet with salt and pepper.
3. Dip the fillet in egg mixture, then bread very lightly.
4. Be sure that your cooking oil (enough to completely cover the fillets) is hot, 375 degrees.
5. Fry the fillets until golden brown. DO NOT OVERCOOK!
6. Brush with melted butter and garnish with a lemon wedge.

Note:

Vary amount of recipe according to number of fish fillets used.

Easy Pickled Fish

WHAT'S NEEDED:

4 cups white vinegar

4 cups cold water

2 large onions, sliced thin

3 Tablespoons pickling spice

1/2 cup salt

1-1/2 cups sugar

fish, skinned and sliced thin (northern pike, walleye, suckers, bullhead)

HERE'S HOW:

1. Combine mixture and pour into a 1 gallon glass jar.
2. Fill to top with thin sliced raw fish.
3. Let stand at room temperature for 48 hours, with lid on loosely.
4. Pour off brine, leaving just enough to cover the fish.
5. Keep in refrigerator indefinitely.

OTHER SAVORIES

OTHER SAVORIES

We have saved this chapter for last. Most of the recipes so far have been entrees or main dishes. Now we'd like to add to your meal.

A couple of reminders. Sauces are ever important. They can make an ordinary meal a feast for the most delicate tastes. Use sauces whenever you can. Also, eye appeal is important. If your food looks good, you do not have to work so hard at convincing your guests or family that it tastes good. Garnishes really come in handy here. Use vibrant colors such as red (cherries), black (olives) and green (parsley). This is a part of your cooking where you can really experiment and be creative.

CAVIAR MOUSSE

WHAT'S NEEDED:

  6 ounces red caviar
  1 teaspoon parsley flakes
  1/4 cup grated fresh onion
  1 teaspoon grated lemon rind
  1 pint sour cream
  1 package gelatin
  1/4 cup hot water
  1 cup whipped cream
  1/4 teaspoon black pepper

HERE'S HOW:

1. Mix the caviar, parsley, onion, lemon rind and sour cream.
2. Mix the gelatin in heated water until it dissolves.
3. Add gelatin, whipped cream and pepper to the other ingredients. Mix well.
4. Place in large mold or individual ones. Refrigerate until set.
5. Serve with rye bread or crackers.

14-16 Servings

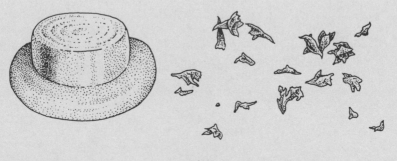

CHEESE STRAWS

WHAT'S NEEDED:

> 1 cup butter, softened
> 2 cups grated sharp Cheddar cheese
> 2-2/3 cups sifted flour
> 1/4 teaspoon salt
> dash paprika
> coarse salt

HERE'S HOW:

1. Mix all ingredients together except coarse salt.
2. Roll dough out to 1/2" thick.
3. Cut into 2" x 1/4" strips.
4. Bake at 275 degrees until light brown.
5. Roll in coarse salt while warm.

Note:
Chilling dough makes this easier to roll.

Yield: 2 dozen

COCKTAIL WIENERS

WHAT'S NEEDED:

> 2 pounds regular or small cocktail wieners
> 1/2 cup chili sauce
> 1-1/4 cups currant jelly
> 2 Tablespoons fresh lemon juice
> 1/4 cup Dijon style mustard

HERE'S HOW:

1. Cut wieners into 1'' pieces.
2. Combine all other ingredients and heat, stirring well.
3. Add wieners and continue heating.
4. Serve hot.

10 Servings

CRABMEAT OR SHRIMP SPREAD

WHAT'S NEEDED:

1/4 cup milk

16 ounces cream cheese (room temperature), cubed

1 Tablespoon lemon juice

2 teaspoons Worcestershire sauce

1 clove garlic, sliced

dash salt and pepper

2 Tablespoons parsley flakes

1 (6-1/2 or 7-1/2 ounce) can crabmeat or shrimp, drained and deveined

HERE'S HOW:

1. Place all ingredients, except crabmeat or shrimp, in blender.
2. Blend at medium speed for 15 seconds, until smooth.
3. Add crabmeat or shrimp.

Yield: 2 cups

DEEP FRIED CAULIFLOWER

WHAT'S NEEDED:

1 package frozen cauliflower buds
hot salted water
1 cup milk
2 eggs
1 teaspoon baking powder
salt and pepper
1 cup flour
seasoned breading
oil for deep frying
melted butter
Parmesan cheese

HERE'S HOW:

1. Thaw the cauliflower in hot salted water by placing on stove and simmer for a few minutes.
2. Drain well, pat cauliflower dry.
3. Mix the milk, eggs, baking powder, salt and pepper and enough flour to make a thick batter.
4. Using a fork, dip cauliflower into the batter allowing surplus batter to run off.
5. Coat with breading.
6. Deep fry at 350 degrees until golden brown.
7. To serve, brush with melted butter and dust with Parmesan cheese.

4-6 Servings

DEEP FRIED MUSHROOMS IN BATTER

WHAT'S NEEDED:

1 large can mushrooms (20-26 count), drained
1/2 teaspoon garlic powder
2 eggs
1 cup milk
2 Tablespoons baking powder
1 cup flour
seasoned breading
oil for deep frying

HERE'S HOW:

1. Dust mushrooms with garlic powder.
2. Mix eggs, milk, baking powder and enough flour to make a thick batter.
3. Using fork, dip mushrooms into batter, allowing surplus batter to run off.
4. Coat with breading.
5. Deep fry at 350 degrees until slightly brown.
6. Serve hot.

14-16 Servings

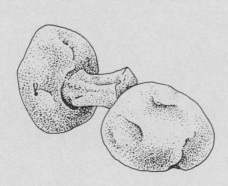

MARINATED MUSHROOMS

WHAT'S NEEDED:

3/4 cup salad oil

1/4 cup olive oil

1/2 cup lemon juice

1 medium onion, chopped fine

1 teaspoon salt

1/4 teaspoon pepper

3 bay leaves

1 teaspoon chopped parsley

1-1/2 cups fresh mushrooms or 3 (4 ounce) cans of
    button mushrooms, drained

HERE'S HOW:

1. Mix together ahead of time to let flavors blend.

12 Servings

POMEGRANATE CHEESE BALLS

WHAT'S NEEDED:

2 (8 ounce) packages cream cheese, softened

1 pound Cheddar cheese, shredded

1/4 pound Roquefort cheese, crumbled

1 or 2 pomegranates

HERE'S HOW:

1. Blend cheeses together until smooth and well
   mixed.
2. Chill until cheeses can be molded, about 30
   minutes.

3. Butter hands and shape cheese into two balls.
4. Cover surface, except bottom, with pomegranate seeds.
5. Wrap in plastic and refrigerate until ready to serve.

Yield: two 4'' balls

OYSTERS ROCKEFELLER

WHAT'S NEEDED:

Butter-spinach mixture:
   1 pound butter, softened
   1 clove garlic
   4 ounces chopped cooked spinach (frozen is fine), squeeze out all the moisture
   2 large green onions or shallots, diced fine
   1 ounce Pernod
4 dozen fresh oysters on the half shell

HERE'S HOW:

1. Place butter-spinach mixture in blender until completely chopped and mixed.
2. Refrigerate for awhile to facilitate handling.
3. Place a tablespoon of butter-spinach mixture on each oyster in the shell and place under broiler until butter is melted and oyster apron starts to curl.

Note:
You may want to crush a few seasoned croutons and use this as a garnish on oysters.

Yield: 4 dozen

SEAFOOD STUFFED PUFF PASTRIES

WHAT'S NEEDED:

1 cup water
1/2 cup butter
1/2 teaspoon salt
1 cup sifted flour
4 eggs
Crabmeat or Shrimp Dip (see index)

HERE'S HOW:

1. Bring water and butter to a boil in a 2 quart pot.
2. Reduce heat to low and add salt and flour.
3. Cook stirring vigorously until mixture leaves side of pot and forms compact ball.
4. Remove from heat, cool slightly.
5. Add eggs one at a time, beating well after each addition.
6. Drop by 1/2 teaspoonful on ungreased cookie sheet and bake 30 minutes until light and dry.
7. When ready to use, cut off tops and fill with Crabmeat or Shrimp Dip.

Yield: 4 dozen

PARMESAN MELT-AROUNDS

WHAT'S NEEDED:

1 cup mayonnaise
1/4 cup Parmesan cheese
1 Tablespoon minced onion
garlic toast rounds

HERE'S HOW:

1. Mix mayonnaise, cheese and onion together.
2. Spread on top of garlic rounds.
3. Put under broiler for a few minutes until cheese bubbles.
4. Serve while warm.

Stuffed Eggs Curry

WHAT'S NEEDED:

1 dozen eggs, hard cooked
1 cup mayonnaise
1 teaspoon chicken stock base
1/4 teaspoon onion powder
1/4 teaspoon white pepper
1 teaspoon curry powder (or more)
1/2 teaspoon salt
tidbits for toppings (capers, anchovies, chopped olives)

HERE'S HOW:

1. Cut hard cooked eggs in half crosswise.
2. Slice a small cap off each end and save.
3. Remove yolk and mash.
4. Add mayonnaise, stock base, onion powder, pepper, curry powder and salt.
5. Mix thoroughly.
6. Refill egg white, piling yolk mixture high.
7. Cap with smaller portion of white and top with tidbits.

Yield: 24

VEGETABLE DIP

WHAT'S NEEDED:

1 package Knorr dry vegetable soup mix
1 pint sour cream

HERE'S HOW:

1. Mix together.
2. Refrigerate for a few hours.
3. Serve with vegetables or chips.

Note:
If too thick, thin with cream.

Yield: 2-1/4 cups

CRABMEAT DIP

WHAT'S NEEDED:

2 (8 ounce) packages cream cheese
1/3 cup mayonnaise
1/2 cup dry white wine
1/4 teaspoon garlic salt or seasoned salt
1-1/2 teaspoons prepared mustard
3/4 teaspoon onion juice
1-1/2 teaspoons confectioners sugar
2 cans crabmeat

HERE'S HOW:

1. Combine cheese, mayonnaise and wine in top of double boiler and heat until blended and smooth.
2. Add remaining ingredients. Serve hot or cold for canapes or as a dip.

Yield: 4 cups

HOT CIDER

WHAT'S NEEDED:

1 quart apple cider
1 pint cranberry juice
1 pint orange juice
1/2 cup sugar
1 teaspoon whole allspice
1 teaspoon whole cloves
3 cinnamon sticks

HERE'S HOW:

1. Put last four items in the perk-basket of your coffee maker.
2. Combine cider and juices in coffee maker and perk until hot.

Yield: 1-1/2 quarts

CHAMPAGNE PUNCH

WHAT'S NEEDED:

2 (12 ounces) cans pineapple juice
1 (6 ounce) can frozen orange juice concentrate, thawed
1 (6 ounce) can frozen lemonade, concentrated
2 bottles champagne, chilled
orange slices

HERE'S HOW:

1. Combine pineapple juice, orange juice, and lemonade, and 4 cups of water.
2. Carefully pour champagne down side of bowl.
3. Stir gently.
4. Garnish with orange slices.

FRUIT PUNCH

WHAT'S NEEDED:

> 4 quarts ginger ale
> 1 quart lime sherbet
> 1 (6 ounce) can orange juice
> 1 (6 ounce) can lemonade

HERE'S HOW:

> 1. Mix together and serve.

Note:
> Can add vodka to taste.

Yield: 5-1/2 quarts

WINE PUNCH

WHAT'S NEEDED:

> 1/2 gallon Sparkling Burgundy
> 1 quart soda water
> 1 cup sugar
> 1 ounce Brandy
> Cointreau, to taste
> orange, lemon and lime slices

HERE'S HOW:

> 1. Combine the above ingredients and place in large bowl.
> 2. Garnish with orange, lemon, and lime slices.

BASIC STUFFING

WHAT'S NEEDED:

1-1/2 cups bread crumbs or commercial stuffing mixture
water
1/4 cup celery, chopped
1/2 cup onions, chopped
1/4 cup butter
1/8 teaspoon poultry seasoning
1/4 teaspoon salt
1/4 teaspoon sage
1 teaspoon chopped parsley

HERE'S HOW:

1. Trim bread, removing crust. Cube. Soak in cold water overnight in an amount enough to cover.
2. Drain. If commercial mix, follow directions.
3. Saute celery and onions in butter until lightly browned.
4. Combine celery, onions, seasonings and bread tossing to blend.
5. Stuff mixture lightly into cavity of fish or poultry to be baked.

Note:

This is a basic stuffing. You may add any variation of your own design. For instance try adding: fresh oysters, raisins, sauteed sausage, fresh diced apple or other fruits, diced ham or diced crisp bacon, or whatever turns you on, including any combination of the above. Don't be afraid to experiment. If you like it, it's good.

Yield: 2-1/4 cups

BAKING POWDER BISCUITS

WHAT'S NEEDED:

4 cups sifted flour
6 teaspoons baking powder
1 teaspoon salt
8 Tablespoons shortening
enough milk to make a stiff dough (about 3/4 cup)

HERE'S HOW:

1. Mix together the flour, baking powder, salt and shortening. Add the milk slowly using only enough to make a very stiff dough.
2. Roll the dough to a thickness approximately 1/2 inch. Cut with a circular cutter (a thin edge water glass works just fine).

3. Place the biscuits on a greased or teflon baking sheet.
4. Bake at 350 degrees approximately 20 minutes or until the biscuits have "popped" and are browned.

Yield: 3 dozen

BEER BATTER

WHAT'S NEEDED:

2 eggs, beaten
12 ounces beer
1-1/2 cups flour
1/4 teaspoon salt
1/4 teaspoon pepper
1/4 teaspoon nutmeg
1/2 teaspoon baking powder
milk, if needed
cornstarch, if needed

HERE'S HOW:

1. Combine beaten eggs and beer.
2. Add dry ingredients all at once.
3. Mix until smooth, adjust consistency as required. (Moisture content of flour may vary. If batter is heavy, adjust with small amount of milk; if batter is too thin, adjust with cornstarch.) Do not overmix.

Yield: 2-1/2 cups

BRAN MUFFINS

WHAT'S NEEDED:

> 1-1/2 cups bran flakes
> 1 cup whole wheat flour
> 1/2 cup raisins (optional)
> 1 teaspoon baking soda
> 1 teaspoon baking powder
> 3/4 cup milk
> 1/2 cup honey or molasses
> 2 Tablespoons oil
> 1 egg, beaten

HERE'S HOW:

1. Stir together bran, flour, raisins, soda and baking powder and set aside.
2. Blend milk, honey, oil and egg and add to dry ingredients.
3. Stir until moistened and spoon into greased muffin pan.
4. Bake 15 minutes at 400 degrees or until muffins pull from side of pan.

Yield: 8-12 muffins

CHERRY BREAD

WHAT'S NEEDED:

> 2 eggs
> 1 cup sugar
> 1-1/2 cups sifted flour
> 1-1/2 Tablespoons baking powder
> 1/2 teaspoon salt
> 1 (8 ounce) jar maraschino cherries, chopped (save juice)
> 1/2 cup chopped nuts

HERE'S HOW:

1. Beat eggs.
2. Cream eggs and sugar until fluffy.
3. Sift in flour, baking powder, salt and juice from jar of cherries.
4. Fold in chopped cherries and nuts.
5. Bake at 350 degrees until brown.

Yield: 1 (4″ x 8″) loaf

CRANBERRY NUT COFFEE CAKE

WHAT'S NEEDED:

1/4 cup brown sugar
1/2 cup chopped walnuts
1/4 teaspoon cinnamon
2 cups Bisquick baking mix
2 Tablespoons sugar
1 egg
2/3 cup water or milk
2/3 cup whole cranberry sauce

HERE'S HOW:

1. Heat oven to 400 degrees. Grease a 9 inch square pan.
2. Mix brown sugar, walnuts, and cinnamon together.
3. Combine baking mix, sugar, egg, and water or milk and beat vigorously $1/2$ minute.
4. Spread dough mixture in pan, sprinkle with nut mixture, spoon cranberry sauce over top.
5. Bake 20-25 minutes. Drizzle with Powdered Sugar Topping (see index) while still warm.

12 Servings

CRANBERRY ORANGE MUFFINS

WHAT'S NEEDED:

- 1/3 cup shortening
- 1/2 cup sugar
- 1 egg
- 1-1/2 cups sifted flour
- 1-1/2 teaspoons baking powder
- 1/2 teaspoon salt
- 1/2 cup milk
- 1/2 jar cranberry orange relish

HERE'S HOW:

1. Mix shortening, sugar and egg thoroughly.
2. Sift dry ingredients together and stir in alternately with milk.
3. Fold in relish.
4. Fill greased muffin tin halfway.
5. Bake at 350 degrees until golden brown.

Note:

Can be put in an egg carton and baked in a microwave.

Yield: 1 dozen

DILLY BREAD

WHAT'S NEEDED:

1 package yeast

1/4 cup warm water

1 cup creamed cottage cheese, heat to lukewarm

2 Tablespoons sugar

1 Tablespoon instant minced onion

1 Tablespoon butter or margarine

4 teaspoons dill seed

1/4 teaspoon soda

1 teaspoon salt

1 unbeaten egg

2-1/4 cups sifted flour

HERE'S HOW:

1. Soften yeast in water.
2. Combine cottage cheese, sugar, onion, butter, dill, soda and salt in saucepan and heat to lukewarm.
3. Add egg and softened yeast to mixture in bowl.
4. Add flour to form stiff dough, beating well.
5. Cover and let rise until size is doubled, approximately 50-60 minutes. Stir down.
6. Pour into greased 8 inch (1½-2 quart) casserole.
7. Let rise for 30-40 minutes.
8. Bake in preheated oven at 350 degrees for 45 minutes.

Yield: 1 round loaf

HOMEMADE BREAD

WHAT'S NEEDED:

2-1/2 cups water
2 cups scalded milk
6 Tablespoons sugar
2 Tablespoons salt
2 packages dry yeast
4 Tablespoons lard
10 cups flour

HERE'S HOW:

1. Add the above ingredients in given order, adding flour gradually.
2. Knead it well.
3. Let dough rest for 10 minutes and then punch down.
4. Let rise about 1½ hours.
5. Divide in four greased pans, and let rise 1-1½ hours.
6. Bake at 350 degrees for 35-45 minutes.

Yield: 4 loaves

HOT CAKES

WHAT'S NEEDED:

3 eggs
3/4 cup sugar
1/4 teaspoon salt
1/4 cup shortening
4 cups milk
4 cups flour
2 Tablespoons baking powder

HERE'S HOW:

1. Mix all ingredients.
2. Let stand at room temperature 30 minutes before using.
3. Wipe heavy skillet with greased cloth and fry using 1/4 cup batter per pancake.
4. Wait till bubbles form all over top, then turn to cook on other side.

Yield: 4 dozen

Hot Popovers

WHAT'S NEEDED:

1-1/2 cups flour
1/4 teaspoon salt
1 pint milk
4 eggs
1 ounce melted butter

HERE'S HOW:

1. Mix all ingredients well with a wire whisk.
2. Do not over beat.
3. Let stand at room temperature for 1 hour.
4. Fill the cups of a teflon coated muffin tin or well greased glass baking dishes, 3/4 full.
5. Bake in a 425 degree oven for approximately 30 minutes or until popovers "pop".

Yield: 10-12

Easy to Make Cinnamon and Caramel Rolls

WHAT'S NEEDED:

> 1 loaf frozen bread dough
>
> 2 Tablespoons melted butter
>
> 1/4 cup white sugar and 1/2 teaspoon cinnamon, mixed together
>
> 1/2 cup brown sugar
>
> Powdered Sugar or Caramel Topping (see below)

HERE'S HOW:

1. Allow frozen bread dough to thaw and rise 4-6 hours in a large, greased bowl.
2. Using a rolling pin, roll the bread dough approximately 1/4 inch thick.
3. Brush with melted butter.
4. Sprinkle liberally with sugar and cinnamon mixture.
5. Spread the brown sugar over the entire area.
6. Roll the dough into a cylinder shape, cut into six equal portions. Place them in a well buttered baking pan dish or individual muffin pan.
7. Place rolls in a warm oven, about 325 degrees for 1 hour or until they have raised approximately 3 inches and are nicely browned.

Yield: 6 rolls

POWDERED SUGAR TOPPING:

To 1/4 cup cold milk, add powdered sugar until you have a very heavy paste. Spoon this over the rolls before serving.

CARAMEL TOPPING:

Before placing the rolls in the baking dish pan, coat the bottom of the pan with 3 Tablespoons melted butter. Sprinkle 1-1/2 cups brown sugar into the pan with the butter. Put the rolls in the pan and follow the same procedure as for the Cinnamon Roll. A few toasted almonds or pecans can be added before putting the rolls in the pan. Invert pan while still warm to remove rolls.

POTATO BUNS

WHAT'S NEEDED:

1 cake yeast
1/2 cup warm water
1 cup potato flakes
1/2 cup sugar
1 teaspoon salt
3/4 cup lard or vegetable shortening
1 cup scalded milk
2 eggs, slightly beaten

HERE'S HOW:

1. Dissolve cake of yeast in 1/2 cup warm water.
2. Combine remaining ingredients and add yeast.
3. Mix into soft dough and set in cool place to rise until light.
4. Roll out 3/4 inch thick and cut with biscuit cutter.
5. Bake at 375 degrees until golden brown.

Yield: 1 dozen

PUMPKIN BREAD

WHAT'S NEEDED:

2/3 cup shortening
3 cups sugar
1 (15 ounce) can pumpkin
4 eggs, well beaten
3-1/2 cups flour
1/2 teaspoon salt
1/2 teaspoon soda
1/2 teaspoon cloves
2 teaspoons cinnamon
1/2 cup chopped nuts (optional)

HERE'S HOW:

1. Cream the shortening and sugar.
2. Add pumpkin and well beaten eggs.
3. Sift together the dry ingredients and stir into pumpkin mixture.
4. Add nuts, if desired.
5. Pour into 3 (4'' x 7'') greased baking pans.
6. Bake at 350 degrees for 1 hour.

Yield: 3 loaves

TROPICAL GINGERBREAD

WHAT'S NEEDED:

1/2 cup shortening
1/2 cup sugar
1 egg
2-1/2 cups sifted all purpose flour
1-1/2 teaspoon baking soda
1 teaspoon cinnamon
1 teaspoon ginger

1/2 teaspoon cloves
1/2 teaspoon salt
1 cup molasses
1 cup hot water

HERE'S HOW:

1. Melt shortening over low heat. Let cool.
2. Add sugar and egg and beat well.
3. Sift together all dry ingredients.
4. Combine molasses and water.
5. Add alternately with the flour to the first mixture.
6. Pour into greased and floured 9 x 9 x 2 pan.
7. Bake in moderate (350 degree) oven until done, or until a toothpick comes out clean when stuck in center.

12 Servings

WELLINGTON PASTRY

WHAT'S NEEDED:

1-1/2 pound flour
1/2 teaspoon salt
3/4 cup butter
3/4 cut shortening
3 egg yolks (save whites)
1 teaspoon olive oil
1 cup cold water

HERE'S HOW:

1. Hand mix all ingredients well. Form ball.
2. Cover and let stand for 1 hour at room temperature.
3. Roll out to 1/8 inch thick and spread with pate as described in Wellington recipes (see index).

SOURDOUGH STARTER

WHAT'S NEEDED:

> 4 cups flour
> 2 teaspoons salt
> 2 Tablespoons sugar
> 3 to 4 cups potato water

HERE'S HOW:

1. Sift the flour, salt and sugar into a large crockery jar. (The mixture will expand.)
2. Add potato water.
3. Let stand for 2 days in a warm area, 90 to 100 degrees. (After it has worked, it will keep 1 week in the refrigerator without reworking it. If left out of refrigerator, it will last 3 days.)
4. To rework starter just add 1 cup warm water and 1 cup sifted flour. (Never add more at one time for each cup of dough than the above and never freeze your starter.)
5. Use as directed for Sourdough Bread.

Note:
If you find you are not using enough starter, take one cup, put it in a pint jar, tie a ribbon around it and give it to a friend.

SOURDOUGH BREAD

WHAT'S NEEDED:

1 cup Sourdough Starter (see index)
1 Tablespoon melted butter
1/4 cup sugar
1/2 teaspoon salt
3 cups flour

HERE'S HOW:

1. Mix Starter, butter, sugar, salt and enough flour to make a soft dough.
2. Knead well.
3. Place in a warm corner until 3 times its size.
4. Toss lightly on a floured board, knead well and shape into a loaf.
5. Place in a greased loaf pan.
6. Let rise until doubled in bulk.
7. Bake at 400 degrees for about 45 minutes.

Yield: 1 loaf

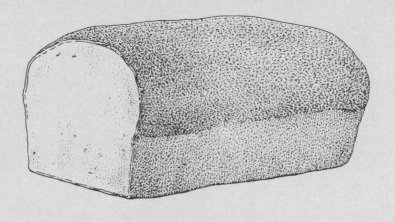

ZUCCHINI BREAD

WHAT'S NEEDED:

1 cup sugar
1/2 cup oil
2 eggs
1 teaspoon grated lemon rind
1/2 teaspoon orange extract
1-1/2 cups flour
2 teaspoons baking powder
1/2 teaspoon soda
1/2 teaspoon salt
1/8 teaspoon nutmeg
1/8 teaspoon ginger
1 cup grated unpeeled zucchini
1/2 cup nuts, chopped (optional)

HERE'S HOW:

1. Beat first five ingredients together.
2. Add sifted dry ingredients alternately with zucchini to sugar mixture.
3. Beat well.
4. Stir in nuts, if desired.
5. Pour into greased 9'' x 5'' loaf pan.
6. Bake at 375 degrees for 55 minutes.
7. Cool 15 minutes in pan.

Yield: 1 loaf

BAKED SPICED APPLES

WHAT'S NEEDED:

1 pint warm water
1/2 pound cinnamon candy (Red Hots)
1 cup sugar
6 apples, cored
whipped cream
chopped walnuts

HERE'S HOW:

1. To 1 pint of warm water, add cinnamon candies and sugar. Stir until candies and sugar are dissolved.
2. Place apples in a baking pan and cover with liquid.
3. Bake in 350 degree oven for 20-30 minutes.
4. Remove from oven. Apples may be served hot or cold.
5. Serve in a dessert dish with some of the liquid.
6. Top with whipped cream and chopped nuts.

6 Servings

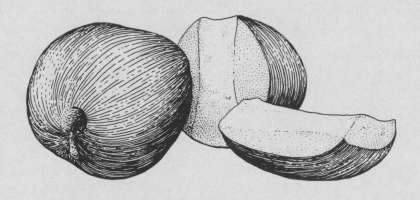

BUTTERSCOTCH PIE

WHAT'S NEEDED:

3/4 cup brown sugar
3 Tablespoons (level) cornstarch
1/2 teaspoon salt
2 cups milk
2 Tablespoons butter
whipped cream
1 8-inch pie shell

HERE'S HOW:

1. Mix together and cook until thick.
2. Cool well and pour into an 8-inch baked pie shell, made either from graham cracker crumbs or a rolled pie crust.
3. Top with whipped cream.

Yield: 1 - 8" pie

CRUMB CRUST

WHAT'S NEEDED:

1-1/4 cups fine crumbs (graham cracker, zweiback, chocolate wafers or gingersnaps)
1/4 cup sugar
1/4 cup softened butter or margarine

HERE'S HOW:

1. Combine ingredients and mix well.
2. Press firmly over bottom and sides of a 9" pie pan.
3. Chill for 1 hour or bake in 375 degree oven for 8 minutes and cool before filling.

Yield: 1 (9") pie shell

CHOCOLATE CHIP PIE

WHAT'S NEEDED:

24 large marshmallows
1/2 cup milk
1/2 pint whipping cream
1 (6 ounce) package of chocolate chips, chopped
1 baked Crumb Crust (see index)

HERE'S HOW:

1. Melt marshmallows with milk in a double boiler until marshmallows are melted. Let cool.
2. Whip the cream until stiff.
3. Beat in the cooled mixture.
4. Fold in chocolate chips.
5. Pour into the Crumb Crust.

Note:

This can either be left plain or crumbs saved from the crust can be sprinkled on top.

Yield: 1 (9'') pie

CHOCOLATE CUTOUTS

For the chocolate lover, you can also serve chocolate cutouts. In double boiler over hot, not boiling, water melt 2 Tablespoons semisweet chocolate pieces and 1 teaspoon butter or margarine; stir until smooth. On waxed paper lined cookie sheet spread chocolate mixture into 6'' x 4'' rectangle. Refrigerate until hard. With chilled cookie cutter cut designs from chocolate rectangle and arrange with chilled spatula on top of frosted cakes, chilled pies, puddings, whipped-cream desserts. Refrigerate until served.

BAKED BANANAS FLAMBE

WHAT'S NEEDED:

>4 large bananas, peeled
>1/2 cup brown sugar
>3 Tablespoons fresh lime juice
>1/4 cup white Rum
>1 teaspoon ground allspice
>butter
>1 Tablespoon 151 proof Rum
>vanilla ice cream (optional)

HERE'S HOW:

1. Cut the bananas lengthwise, then in half across.
2. Arrange in a well buttered baking dish.
3. Sprinkle with sugar, lime juice, white Rum and allspice.
4. Dot with butter.
5. Bake at 350 degrees for 30 minutes, basting occasionally during baking time.
6. Just before serving, heat the 151 proof Rum. Pour over the bananas and flame.
7. Serve plain or over vanilla ice cream.

6-8 Servings

MINIATURE CHEESE CAKES

WHAT'S NEEDED:

>3 dozen vanilla wafers
>midget baking cups
>2 (8 ounce) packages cream cheese, softened
>3/4 cup sugar
>2 eggs
>1 teaspoon lemon juice
>1 teaspoon vanilla extract
>1 can blueberry or cherry pie filling

HERE'S HOW:

1. Place 1 vanilla wafer in each baking cup in muffin tins.
2. Beat remaining ingredients, except pie filling, with mixer at high speed until fluffy (about 5 minutes).
3. Fill baking cups 2/3 full.
4. Bake at 350 degrees for 15-20 minutes.
5. Cool and top with fruit pie filling.

Yield: 3 dozen

SALAD DRESSING CAKE

WHAT'S NEEDED:

1 cup salad dressing

1 cup sugar

2 cups flour

2 teaspoons baking soda

4 Tablespoons cocoa

1 cup warm water

1 teaspoon vanilla

dash of salt

HERE'S HOW:

1. Combine above ingredients.
2. Place in 9 x 13 baking pan and bake at 350 degrees for 35-40 minutes.

16 Servings

GRASSHOPPER PIE

WHAT'S NEEDED:

6 ounces lime gelatin (Jello)
4 Tablespoons sugar
1/4 teaspoon salt
2 cups boiling water
3/4 cup cold water
1/3 cup Creme de Cocoa
1/3 cup Creme de Menthe
1 teaspoon vanilla
1 egg white
1 envelope Dream Whip, whipped or 1 cup whipping cream
9'' Crumb Crust (see index)
chocolate curls

HERE'S HOW:

1. Dissolve gelatin, 2 Tablespoons sugar and salt in boiling water.
2. Add cold water, liqueurs and vanilla. Mix well.
3. Chill until slightly thickened.
4. Beat egg white until foamy.
5. Gradually add remaining sugar, beating after each addition until well blended and forms a meringue that stands in shiny soft peaks.
6. Prepare whipped topping, mix as directed on package (omitting vanilla) or whip the whipping cream.
7. Measure 1/2 cup gelatin and set aside.
8. Blend meringue and prepared topping into remaining gelatin.
9. Chill until quite thick.

10. Spoon into Crumb Crust, using as much as possible. (Any remaining filling may be chilled in sherbet glasses.)
11. Drizzle the reserved clear gelatin over the top of the pie, pulling a spoon over the pie through a zig-zag course to create a marble effect.
12. Chill until firm.
13. Garnish with chocolate curls.

Yield: 1 (9") pie

ICE BOX COOKIES

WHAT'S NEEDED:

1/2 cup chopped walnuts or pecans
1/2 cup shortening (part butter)
1 cup brown sugar
1 egg
1/2 teaspoon vanilla
1/2 teaspoon soda
1/4 teaspoon salt
1-1/2 cups flour

HERE'S HOW:

1. Combine the above ingredients.
2. Form into a roll — like a jelly roll — wrap in waxed paper, and refrigerate for about 3 hours to overnight.
3. Slice thin and bake on a greased cookie sheet at 350-375 degrees for 8 to 10 minutes.

ORANGES IN WINE SAUCE

WHAT'S NEEDED:

3/4 cup sugar

1 cup water

1 cup dry red wine

2 whole cloves

1 stick of cinnamon

1 vanilla bean

1/2 lemon, sliced

6 large seedless oranges, peeled (including all white tissue membrane) and sliced

HERE'S HOW:

1. Mix all ingredients except the oranges in a sauce pan and simmer for 5 minutes.
2. Pour the sauce over the sliced oranges and refrigerate for 4-5 hours before using.

6-8 Servings

PEARS A LA COLLINS

WHAT'S NEEDED:

1 (# 2-1/2) can Bartlett pears

2 ounces green Creme de Menthe

1/2 ounce white Creme de Cocoa

whipped cream

maraschino cherries

chopped pecans

HERE'S HOW:

1. Remove the pears and juice to a crock.
2. Add liqueur to pears. Refrigerate for 1 hour.
3. Serve in individual dessert dishes with a little of the liquid.
4. Fill pear cavity with whipped cream, cherries and top with chopped pecans.

8 Servings

PEAR SHERBET

WHAT'S NEEDED:

1 (16 ounce) can Bartlett pear halves, drained (save juice)
1 quart liquid from canned pears
juice of 2 lemons
1/2 cup granulated sugar
1/4 cup pear Brandy
8 canned Bartlett pear halves
1/4 cup Kummel liqueur

HERE'S HOW:

1. Blend the first 4 ingredients in a blender until the mixture reaches a sherbet consistency (about 15 minutes).
2. Add the pear Brandy.
3. Place in freezer until serving time.
4. Place chilled pear halves, cut side up, in a sherbet glass.
5. Spoon the sherbet into the hollow of the pear.
6. Top with a teaspoon of ice cold Kummel.

8 Servings

RUSSIAN MINT PIES

WHAT'S NEEDED:

1 cup butter or margarine
2 cups powdered sugar
4 eggs
4 ounces unsweetened chocolate, melted
1 teaspoon peppermint extract
1 teaspoon vanilla extract
1 cup crushed vanilla wafers
whipped topping
cherries

HERE'S HOW:

1. Cream the butter and sugar.
2. Add eggs, one at a time, beating each about 5 minutes.
3. Add chocolate, peppermint and vanilla.
4. Spoon half of the crumbs in bottom of paper lined cupcake tins.
5. Pour chocolate mixture on top of the crumbs.
6. Cover with remaining crumbs.
7. Dab whipping cream on top of each cup and add a cherry.
8. Chill and serve.

Note:
These will keep well frozen for several weeks.

Yield: 15-16

FROSTED MINT LEAVES

WHAT'S NEEDED:

mint leaves
1 egg white, beaten
2 drops peppermint extract
1 cup sugar

HERE'S HOW:

1. Remove stems from mint leaves, coat both sides with egg white.
2. Combine peppermint and sugar, dip leaves in mixture, coating well.
3. Place on waxed paper or in slow oven to dry.

Note:
A good garnish for fruit salads or desserts.

CANDY COATED NUTS

WHAT'S NEEDED:

3 egg whites, beaten stiff
1 cup sugar
1/2 cup butter
1 pound can mixed nuts (or two 12 ounce cans)

HERE'S HOW:

1. Gradually add sugar to beaten egg whites and beat until stiff.
2. Melt butter on jelly roll pan.
3. Coat nuts with sugar mixture, place on pan spreading evenly.
4. Bake in a 325 degree oven for 30 minutes. Stir with fork every 10 minutes.
5. Cool and break into pieces.

Yield: 1 pound

CARROT BARS

WHAT'S NEEDED:

2 cups flour
2 cups white sugar
2 teaspoons baking soda
4 eggs
1-1/2 teaspoons cinnamon
1 cup salad oil
2 jars Jr. carrot baby food

HERE'S HOW:

1. Mix all ingredients together.
2. Place in lightly greased jelly roll pan.
3. Bake at 350 degrees for 30 minutes. Cool.
4. Top with frosting and cut into squares.

FROSTING

WHAT'S NEEDED:

2 cups powdered sugar
2 teaspoons vanilla
6 ounces cream cheese, softened
1/2 cup margarine, softened
1/2 cup chopped nuts

HERE'S HOW:

1. Mix all ingredients well.
2. Spread over cooled carrot bars.

Rum Balls

WHAT'S NEEDED:

1 cup fine dry cookie, cake or vanilla wafer crumbs
1 cup powdered sugar
2 Tablespoons cocoa
1/2   teaspoon ground cinnamon
1/2   teaspoon ground ginger
1 cup chopped nuts
2 Tablespoons corn syrup
1/4   cup Rum
powdered sugar

HERE'S HOW:

1. Combine crumbs, powdered sugar, cocoa, cinnamon, ginger and nuts. Mix well.
2. Stir in syrup and Rum.
3. Shape into 1 inch balls with hands lightly dusted with powdered sugar.
4. Roll balls in sifted powdered sugar.

Note:
You may store these in covered jars in the refrigerator until ready to serve.

Yield: 30 balls

TURTLES

WHAT'S NEEDED:

> 12 ounces semi-sweet or sweet chocolate chips
> 1 large bag of caramels or Wrapples
> 8 ounces pecan or walnut halves

HERE'S HOW:

1. Melt the chocolate in a double boiler.
2. Melt the caramels and pour on top of 3 pecan or walnut halves that have been placed together on wax paper. (If using Wrapples, cut a square and place on top of nut groupings.)
3. Let cool to set.
4. Dip in melted chocolate until well covered.

Yield: 6 dozen

DILLED BEANS

WHAT'S NEEDED:

3 pounds whole green beans
6 cloves garlic, peeled
6 dill heads or 2 Tablespoons dill seed
1-1/2 teaspoons cayenne pepper
3-1/4 cups water
3-1/4 cups dark vinegar
6 Tablespoons salt (coarse or pickling)

HERE'S HOW:

1. Wash beans, cut off ends.
2. Pack lengthwise in clean pint jars, leaving 1/4''-1/2'' of headroom.
3. Add 1 clove garlic, 1 head of dill or 1 teaspoon dill seed and 1/4 teaspoon cayenne to each pint jar.
4. Mix the water, vinegar and salt togehter in an enamel kettle.
5. Bring it to a boil and pour over the beans in the jars.
6. Leave 1/4 inch headroom, cover and tighten lids.
7. Boil for 10 minutes with each jar covered over top with 1 inch water.
8. Store at room temperature for 2 weeks for full flavor to develop.

Yield: 6 pints

KRAUT RELISH

WHAT'S NEEDED:

> 2 cups canned sauerkraut, drained
> 2 cups canned bean sprouts, drained
> 1 green pepper, chopped
> 2 cups chopped celery
> 2 cups diced onion
> 2 cups sugar
> 1 cup white wine vinegar
> 1/4 cup chopped pimento

HERE'S HOW:

1. Mix all ingredients together.
2. Place in covered container and "let work" in refrigerator.
3. Keeps well.

Yield: 2 quarts

MARINATED VEGETABLES

WHAT'S NEEDED:

> 1/2 cup white wine vinegar
> 1/4 cup vegetable oil
> 3/4 teaspoon salt
> 1/2 teaspoon oregano
> dash of pepper
> 2 tomatoes, peeled and diced
> 2 cucumbers, peeled and sliced
> 1 medium onion, peeled and sliced
> 1/4 cup sliced Greek or ripe olives
> shredded lettuce

HERE'S HOW:

1. Combine vinegar, oil, salt, oregano and pepper in a jar, cover and shake vigorously.
2. Combine vegetables and olives in a bowl. Add vinegar mixture.
3. Cover and marinate several hours in refrigerator.
4. Serve on top of shredded lettuce.

Yield: 5 cups

ZUCCHINI TOSS

WHAT'S NEEDED:

1 head lettuce, washed and chilled
1 small bunch romaine, washed and chilled
1/4 cup olive oil
2 medium zucchini, thinly sliced
1 cup sliced radishes
3 green onions, sliced
3 Tablespoons blue cheese crumbled
2 Tablespoons tarragon or white vinegar
3/4 teaspoon salt
1 small clove garlic, crushed
1/4 teaspoon MSG (optional)
generous dash freshly ground pepper

HERE'S HOW:

1. Into large bowl, tear greens into bite size pieces.
2. Toss with oil until leaves glisten.
3. Add zucchini, radishes, onions, and cheese.
4. Combine vinegar, salt, garlic, MSG (if used) and pepper.
5. Pour over salad mixture and toss.

6-8 Servings

AMANDINE SAUCE

WHAT'S NEEDED:

>6 Tablespoons butter
>1 teaspoon fresh lemon juice
>dash of cayenne
>dash of paprika
>1 teaspoon sliced almonds

HERE'S HOW:

>1. Melt butter in sauce pan. Add lemon, cayenne, paprika and almonds.
>2. Saute on medium heat until almonds are golden brown.
>3. Spoon hot sauce over broiled or fried fish fillet.

Yield: 1/2 cup

BARBECUE SAUCE

WHAT'S NEEDED:

>1 Tablespoon butter, melted
>1 cup ketchup
>3/4 cup water
>2 Tablespoons brown sugar
>2 Tablespoons lemon juice
>2 Tablespoons vinegar
>1 teaspoon dry mustard
>salt, pepper and dry onion flakes (as desired)

HERE'S HOW:

>1. Mix ingredients together well.
>2. Heat and use as basting for ribs and other barbecued meats and fowl.

Yield: 2 cups

Basic Cream Sauce

WHAT'S NEEDED:

1/2 pound butter
4 cups flour
2 cups water
2 cups milk
5 chicken bouillon cubes
salt and pepper
yellow food coloring

HERE'S HOW:

1. Prepare a butter roux by heating the butter over a slightly higher than medium heat until it foams. However, be careful not to scorch the butter or your roux will be dark and discolored.
2. Slowly add flour, stirring constantly with a wire whisk, until flour-butter mixture loses its bright sheen and acquires a dull appearance. The consistency at this point will be almost solid. Remove from heat. (This mixture may be stored in a refrigerator for an extended period of time.)
3. Mix the milk and water and heat. Dissolve the bouillon cubes into this mixture.
4. Season to taste with salt and pepper Heat very hot, but *do not boil.*
5. Thicken mixture by adding small amounts of butter roux while stirring continuously with a wire whisk, until it reaches a medium thick consistency. Remove from heat.
6. A drop of yellow food coloring may be added.

Yield: 8 cups

BORDELAISE SAUCE

WHAT'S NEEDED:

1 clove garlic, diced to a pulp
1 green onion, diced fine
1/2 teaspoon paprika
1 cup Beef Stock (see index)
cornstarch or arrowroot and water

HERE'S HOW:

1. Place the garlic, onion and paprika in a heavy sauce pan.
2. Heat over high heat, stirring constantly until the paprika turns a deep dark red. Do not burn.
3. Add the Beef Stock.
4. Thicken slightly with paste made from cornstarch or arrowroot and water.
5. Serve very hot over your favorite meat.

Yield: 1 cup

BRANDIED PEACH SAUCE

WHAT'S NEEDED:

2 cups canned pitted peaches (1-#303 can), with juice
juice of 1/2 fresh lemon
1 cup sugar
1 ounce Peach Brandy
dash of ground cloves

HERE'S HOW:

1. Blend the peaches and juice with lemon juice, sugar, Brandy and a dash of cloves in a blender.
2. Bring to a boil in a sauce pan. This should thicken it somewhat. If it isn't sufficiently thick, add a paste made of cornstarch or arrowroot and water.
3. Serve hot on top of waterfowl or upland game birds.
4. May be used as a glaze on any fowl.

Yield: 2-1/2 cups

BRANDIED APRICOT SAUCE

WHAT'S NEEDED:

2 cups canned pitted apricots (1-#303 can), with juice
juice of 1/2 fresh lemon
1 cup sugar
1 ounce Apricot Brandy
dash ground cloves

HERE'S HOW:

1. Blend the apricots and juice, sugar, Brandy and dash of cloves in a blender.
2. Bring to a boil in a sauce pan. This should thicken it somewhat. If it isn't sufficiently thick, add a paste made of cornstarch or arrowroot and water.

Yield: 2-1/2 cups

CHERRY SAUCE

WHAT'S NEEDED:

3 cups maraschino cherry juice
1 cup dry Sherry
1/2 cup brown sugar
1/4 cup concentrated lemon juice
3 to 4 ounces Southern Comfort liqueur

HERE'S HOW:

1. Blend all ingredients in blender until well mixed.
2. Heat, but do not boil.
3. Serve hot over goose or duck.

Yield: 5 cups

COLLINS TARTAR SAUCE

WHAT'S NEEDED:

1 pint salad dressing
3 teaspoons capers
1/2 cup finely diced stuffed olives
1/2 cup finely diced onions
juice of 1/2 fresh lemon
dash of cayenne (optional)

HERE'S HOW:

1. Mix all ingredients together well.
2. Refrigerate until needed.
3. Serve with your favorite fish.

Yield: 1-1/2 pints

CUMBERLAND SAUCE

WHAT'S NEEDED:

1 pint beef or game stock
1 cup red currant jelly
1/2 cup brown sugar
3 ounces Creme de Cassis
dash of cayenne
2 teaspoons medium dry mustard
2 oranges
2 lemons
cornstarch or arrowroot and water

HERE'S HOW:

1. Place all ingredients, except oranges and lemons, in a sauce pan.
2. Grate the rinds from the oranges and lemons.
3. Place the grated peel in a separate sauce pan with 1 inch of water and bring to a boil.
4. Drain thoroughly and add to sauce.
5. Juice the oranges and lemons and add juice to sauce. Heat the sauce to boiling and thicken with a paste made from cornstarch or arrowroot and water.
6. Serve with boar or caribou.

Yield: 3 cups

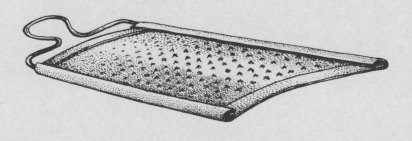

CREOLE SAUCE

WHAT'S NEEDED:

2-1/2 Tablespoons salad oil
1/4 cup diced onions
1/4 cup diced celery
1/2 clove garlic, crushed
1 (12 ounce) can tomatoes, crushed
1 (4 ounce) can tomato puree
dash of thyme
1 bay leaf
dash of black pepper
salt
1/2 cup green pepper, diced
cayenne pepper

HERE'S HOW:
1. Heat oil in sauce pan.
2. Add onions, celery and garlic. Saute until golden brown.
3. Add canned tomatoes and tomato puree and seasonings. Simmer at very low heat for 30 minutes.
4. Blanch green peppers in salted boiling water for 6 minutes. Drain.
5. When sauce is cooked, remove bay leaf and add green pepper.
6. Check seasoning for taste.
7. Use with fish or meat.

Yield: 2 cups

GINGER SAUCE

WHAT'S NEEDED:

1/2 cup soy sauce
1/4 cup vinegar
1 medium onion, peeled and sliced
1 large clove garlic, peeled
1/4 teaspoon powdered ginger or fresh peeled grated
   ginger
1/2 ounce Ginger Brandy (optional)

HERE'S HOW:

1. Blend all ingredients in a blender until thoroughly mixed.
2. Heat (but do not boil) before serving.

Note:
The sauce may also be served cold.

Yield: 1 cup

MAITRE D'HOTEL SAUCE

WHAT'S NEEDED:

6 Tablespoons butter, melted
1 Tablespoon fresh lemon juice
dash of Cognac

HERE'S HOW:

1. Mix melted butter, lemon juice and Cognac.
2. Serve hot.

Yield: 1/2 cup

HORSERADISH SAUCE

WHAT'S NEEDED:

1/2 pint mayonnaise
1/2 pint sour cream
1 Tablespoon chopped chives or green onions
1 Tablespoon horseradish
juice of 1/4 fresh lemon

HERE'S HOW:

1. Mix mayonnaise, sour cream, horseradish, chives and lemon juice.
2. Store the sauce in a covered container in refrigerator for 2 hours.
3. Serve with thinly sliced game meat.

Yield: 1 pint

MEUNIERE SAUCE

WHAT'S NEEDED:

1/2 cup butter
1 teaspoon chopped fresh parsley
1 teaspoon fresh lemon juice

HERE'S HOW:

1. Heat 1/2 cup butter in a saucepan until browned.
2. Sprinkle fish with chopped parsley.
3. Mix lemon juice with browned butter, pour over fish.

4 Servings

HOLLANDAISE SAUCE

WHAT'S NEEDED:

6 egg yolks
2 Tablespoons cold water
1 pound clarified butter, warmed
juice of 1 fresh lemon
dash of cayenne pepper
dash of salt

HERE'S HOW:

1. With wire whisk, mix egg yolks and water in top of double boiler over medium heat.
2. Stir the eggs lightly until slightly thickened.
3. Remove from heat and allow to cool 10-15 minutes. Stir occasionally.
4. Whip the warm butter into eggs and season with lemon, cayenne and salt.
5. Serve warm.

Yield: 2 cups

MUSTARD SAUCE

WHAT'S NEEDED:

> 1/4 cup medium dry mustard
> 1/4 cup water
> 2 Tablespoons heavy cream
> 1/2 cup soy sauce
> 1 Tablespoon sesame seeds
> 1 teaspoon grated lemon rind

HERE'S HOW:

1. Mix ingredients well with a wire whisk.
2. Refrigerate and allow to stand 1 hour before using.
3. Serve with or over cold roast leg of wild boar or other game.

> **Yield: 1 cup**

ORANGE PINEAPPLE SAUCE

WHAT'S NEEDED:

> 1 cup pineapple juice
> 1 cup sugar
> 1 ounce Grand Marnier
> dash of ground cloves

HERE'S HOW:

1. Mix the ingredients and bring to boil. Stir regularly so it does not scorch.
2. The mixture should thicken somewhat. However, if it remains too thin, thicken it a bit with a paste made of cornstarch and water.

> **Yield: 1-1/2 cups**

Sauce for Fresh Fruit

WHAT'S NEEDED:

1/4 pound butter, melted and cooled
2 cups powdered sugar
1 egg
1-1/2 ounce Blackberry Brandy
1 cup whipped cream

HERE'S HOW:

1. Whip the first 3 ingredients together.
2. Refrigerate for 4 hours.
3. Remove from refrigerator and add Brandy and whipped cream.
4. Use with fresh fruit or fruit salads.

Yield: 2 cups

Sweet Sauce

WHAT'S NEEDED:

2 oranges
4 ounces Sherry
3 Tablespoons prepared mustard
1 cup plum jelly

HERE'S HOW:

1. Grate oranges.
2. Place grated orange rind in saucepan with 1/2 inch water.
3. Bring to boil for 2 minutes, drain.
4. Add blanched grated orange peel to Sherry, mustard and jelly.

Yield: 1-1/2 cups

SPAGHETTI SAUCE

WHAT'S NEEDED:

1 pound browned ground meat
3 (#2-1/2) cans crushed tomatoes
3 (8 ounce) cans tomato sauce
3 (6 ounce) cans tomato paste
2 teaspoons finely minced garlic
3 teaspoons sugar
2 teaspoons crushed oregano
2 teaspoons Accent (optional)
1 medium onion, diced
1 teaspoon sweet basil
6 Tablespoons diced green pepper
1 (8 ounce) can mushrooms
salt and pepper to taste
Parmesan cheese

HERE'S HOW:

1. Mix all ingredients together in large pot, omitting the cheese.
2. Simmer on low heat for about 1 hour, stirring occasionally.
3. Pour over cooked pasta and top with Parmesan Cheese.

8-10 Servings

Note:
You may leave out the meat for a meatless sauce. Either way it can be stored in the refrigerator for several days or frozen for future use.

TOMATO SAUCE

WHAT'S NEEDED:

- 1/8 teaspoon minced garlic
- 1/8 cup finely chopped onion
- 1/8 cup finely chopped celery
- 1/4 cup melted butter
- 1 (16 ounce) can tomato sauce
- 1/8 teaspoon thyme
- 1/4 teaspoon sweet basil
- dash of powdered cloves
- salt and pepper
- dash of cayenne

HERE'S HOW:

1. Saute garlic, onion and celery in butter until golden brown.
2. Add tomato sauce and seasonings.
3. Simmer for 15 minutes.
4. Pour over the fish to be baked.
5. Baste several times with sauce while baking.

Yield: 2 cups

TARRAGON SAUCE

WHAT'S NEEDED:

2 cups mayonnaise
1 cup sour cream
1/4 cup sweet cream
1/2 teaspoon tarragon vinegar
2-3 drops Bitters
1/2 teaspoon dried tarragon leaves

HERE'S HOW:

1. Mix ingredients well with a wire whisk.
2. Refrigerate for 1 hour before using.
3. Serve with cold game meats.

Yield: 3 cups

BROWN GRAVY

WHAT'S NEEDED:

4 cups Beef Stock (see index)
2 Tablespoons tomato paste
4 bouillon cubes

HERE'S HOW:

1. Combine ingredients in a sauce pan and bring to a boil.
2. Gradually thicken with small amounts of Lard Roux (see index).

Note:
Flavor may be altered by adding 1-1/2 ounces of Sherry wine.

WILD GAME MARINADE

WHAT'S NEEDED:

1 bottle Burgundy wine

1 cup red wine vinegar

3 large onions, peeled and sliced

1/2 teaspoon whole black peppercorns or 1/4 teaspoon black pepper

1/2 teaspoon whole cloves

1/2 teaspoon Juniper berries

1/2 teaspoon thyme

1 teaspoon salt

3 Tablespoons chopped parsley

3 bay leaves

HERE'S HOW:

1. Combine the marinade ingredients, mixing well.
2. Pour over the meat in glass or enamel bowl.
3. Cover and refrigerate for 24 hours, or 2-3 days for large roasts.
4. Turn the meat occasionally to expose all surfaces to marinade.
5. Remove the meat from marinade and prepare in any desired manner.

Yield: 5-1/2 cups

CREAM SOUPS

You can make any flavored cream soup that you wish by simply preparing a very light chicken stock based Cream Sauce (see index), and adding to it whatever fires your imagination. Here's an example:

WHAT'S NEEDED:

> 1 pint whole milk
> 1 pint water
> Butter Roux (see index)
> 1 cup canned, cut asparagus spears
> 1 teaspoon chicken bouillon granules
> 1/8 teaspoon black pepper
> 1/4 teaspoon MSG or Accent (optional)
> yellow food coloring

HERE'S HOW:

1. The cardinal rule is this: "Everything has to be hot to hang together."
2. Heat the milk and the water separately. Do not boil the milk, but it should be very hot.
3. Thicken the milk with the Butter Roux until a very heavy paste is formed. (Do this over moderate heat, stirring constantly as the roux is added a bit at a time.)
4. Add the thickened milk to the hot water.
5. Add the asparagus spears, bouillon granules, pepper and MSG (optional) to the soup.
6. Whip well with a wire whisk.

Note:
You may find that a couple drops of yellow food coloring will enhance the appearance of this soup. Instead of using asparagus, try some of the following suggestions:
1. Add cooked broccoli, cooked cauliflower buds,

chopped spinach, or any other vegetable that appeals to you.
2. Add grated Cheddar cheese.
3. Add diced cooked chicken, turkey, pheasant or any wild fowl.
4. Add diced smoked fowl, fish or canned salmon.
5. Add chopped hard boiled egg.
6. Add sliced roasted almonds.
7. Add combinations of the above.

BUTTER ROUX

Butter Roux will keep refrigerated for an extended period of time, so if you're going to do a bit of cooking now and then, don't be afraid to cook up a batch. This roux is used primarily for thickening vegetable or chicken flavored sauces and soups.

WHAT'S NEEDED:

> **butter**
> **flour**

HERE'S HOW:

> The amount of butter will depend on the amount of roux you choose to make. You can make as little or as much as you wish. The procedure remains the same.
> 1. Heat the butter (perhaps a pound or less) in a heavy saucepan at medium heat until it foams. Do not scorch the butter.
> 2. Slowly add flour, whipping constantly with a wire whisk until the butter has absorbed enough flour to have lost its "gloss" or shine. At this point roux will be almost solid.

Note:
This roux is used to thicken cream sauces and "white" stocks for chicken, fish, etc.

BEEF STOCK

WHAT'S NEEDED:

1 (3-4 pound) roast of any game meat or beef, preferably
   with bone in
salt and pepper
paprika
1/2 medium onion, peeled
3 cloves garlic, peeled
tops from one rib of celery
2 carrots, peeled
1/4 teaspoon whole pickling spice
2 quarts hot water

HERE'S HOW:

1. Place the roast, vegetables and spices in a baking
   pan or roaster.
2. Season the roast with salt and pepper. Dust
   lavishly with paprika.
3. Bake uncovered at 350 degrees for approximately
   1 hour.
4. Add 2 quarts of hot water. Continue to bake for
   another 30-40 minutes.
5. Remove the roast. Strain the stock.
6. To give this stock the extra zip that you may
   want, you can either add 3 or 4 beef bouillon
   cubes or reduce the stock by simmering uncovered at low heat to approximately one half of its
   volume. Before using the stock, you may want
   to add a bit more salt for seasoning and 1 ounce
   of tomato paste per quart of stock for color. This
   isn't really necessary, but it *is* better.

French Onion Soup

This recipe is so simple that I hesitate to give it out, but everyone who has it has liked it so much; they always ask for the recipe!

WHAT'S NEEDED:

> 1/4 cup margarine
> 3 onions, either sliced thinly or diced coarsely
> 1 (#2-1/2) can beef consomme
> 1/2 (#2-1/2) can water
> 1/2 (#2-1/2) can dry white wine
> bread slices
> Swiss cheese slices

HERE'S HOW:

1. Melt margarine, add sliced or diced onions and simmer until onions are tender.
2. Add consomme, water, and dry white wine and simmer $\frac{1}{2}$ hour.
3. Pour into a baking soup crock, layer with bread slice, then two layers of Swiss cheese.
4. Bake at 350 degrees until cheese melts.

4 Servings

CHICKEN BASED STOCK

If you want your chicken based stocks to get appreciative "oohs and ahs" from your guests, you are going to have to use real chicken.

WHAT'S NEEDED:

> 1 fat stewing hen
> 1 medium onion, peeled
> top from one rib of celery
> 2 carrots, peeled
> salt and pepper
> 1-1/2 gallons water

HERE'S HOW:

1. Place all ingredients in a large pot with water.
2. Bring to a boil, reduce heat and simmer, covered, for approximately 2 hours or until chicken is completely tender.
3. Remove the chicken and strain the stock to remove the celery and onions.
4. Return the stock to the pot and simmer uncovered at low heat until it is reduced to approximately 3 quarts, or you can use 3 or 4 chicken bouillon cubes as a "booster".
5. Make sandwiches out of the cold chicken.

LARD BASE ROUX OR WHITE ROUX

This roux is used primarily for thickening meat flavored sauces or gravies as it will retain and enhance meat flavors. This roux will keep almost indefinitely if refrigerated, and you will find frequent uses for it.

WHAT'S NEEDED:

> lard
> flour

HERE'S HOW:

1. Heat whatever amount of lard you wish to use (perhaps a pound or less) in a heavy saucepan. It should be very, very hot but not "smoking" hot.
2. Carefully add flour, stirring constantly and rapidly with a wire whisk until maximum amount of flour has been absorbed into the lard, and its glossiness has dulled.
3. Reduce your heat to low and allow to "cook" for a few minutes. This will remove the flour taste.

Note:

Extreme caution should be used in the preparation of this roux. Adding flour to the hot lard will cause a great deal of foaming and sputtering. Therefore, add the flour slowly, whipping constantly.

BEAN SALAD

WHAT'S NEEDED:

1-1/2 cups sugar

1/2 cup salad oil

1 cup vinegar

1 teaspoon salt

1/2 teaspoon black pepper

1 teaspoon celery seed

1 teaspoon mustard seed

salt and pepper to taste

2 cups each of canned cut green beans, yellow beans, kidney beans and lima beans, drained

1 large onion, peeled and sliced

1 green pepper, diced into 1/4'' pieces

1 sweet red pepper, diced into 1/4'' pieces

HERE'S HOW:

1. Bring the first eight ingredients to a boil. Remove from heat and cool.
2. Mix remaining ingredients together.
3. Pour cooled liquid over bean mixture.
4. Stir and refrigerate covered, 12 to 24 hours.
5. Serve cold. It will keep indefinitely.

Yield: 3 quarts

DEEP FRIED POTATO BALLS

WHAT'S NEEDED:

4 boiled potatoes, peeled and grated

2 eggs

1/2 teaspoon baking powder

1/2 cup milk

1/2 cup flour
1/2 cup grated cheese (optional)
salt and pepper
fat for frying

HERE'S HOW:

1. Mix all ingredients together well.
2. Season with salt and pepper to taste.
3. Form into 1 inch balls.
4. Deep fry in 350 degree fat.

Yield: 2 dozen

DUMPLINGS

WHAT'S NEEDED:

3 heaping teaspoons baking powder
3 cups flour
1 cup milk
3 eggs, beaten slightly
dash of salt
dash of mace
Beef or Chicken Stock (see index)

HERE'S HOW:

1. Baking powder and flour must be triple sifted.
2. Mix all ingredients together well.
3. Place 1 teaspoon of dough for each dumpling on a steamer rack.
4. Steam over beef or chicken stock until dumplings are cooked through.

4-6 Servings

HUNTING CAMP BAKED BEANS

WHAT'S NEEDED:

2 pounds great northern beans
1 medium onion, diced fine
4 cloves garlic, diced very fine
8 strips bacon, chopped
1 cup sugar
salt and pepper

HERE'S HOW:

1. Soak beans in cold water overnight.
2. Drain beans thoroughly. Add onion, garlic, bacon and sugar. Salt and pepper to taste.
3. Mix well and place in casserole.
4. Bake covered in 325 degree oven until beans are tender, about 1 hour.

8-10 Servings

WILD RICE CUMBERLAND

WHAT'S NEEDED:

3 cups cooked Wild Rice (see index)
grated rind of 2 oranges, blanched
2 ounces red currant jelly
1/2 ounce Creme de Cassis
1/4 teaspoon black pepper
1/2 teaspoon granulated chicken bouillon

HERE'S HOW:

1. Mix all ingredients together thoroughly.
2. Serve very hot.

Yield: 3 cups

WILD RICE DRESSING

WHAT'S NEEDED:

1 cup wild rice
1 quart water
1/2 teaspoon salt
1 chicken bouillon cube
1/4 cup butter
1 rib celery, diced
1/4 medium onion, diced
1/4 cup canned mushrooms (stems and pieces)
salt
white pepper
1 slice canned pimento, diced

HERE'S HOW:

1. Place rice, water, 1/2 teaspoon salt, bouillon cube in covered sauce pan and boil on medium heat until water is absorbed and rice is tender and fluffy, about 30 minutes.
2. In a separate fry pan, melt 1/8 cup butter, add celery, onion, mushrooms and saute until golden.
3. Add this mixture to boiled rice.
4. Season with salt and pepper to taste.
5. Add pimento and remaining 1/8 cup butter.
6. Mix well and serve.

6-8 Servings

WILD RICE OR WHITE RICE

Don't be afraid of wild rice. Cook the same as raw white rice.

WHAT'S NEEDED:

> 1 cup wild or white rice
> 3 cups cold water
> 1 teaspoon chicken bouillon granules or 1/2 teaspoon salt
> 2 Tablespoons butter

HERE'S HOW:

1. In a 2 quart sauce pan, cover rice with water. Add bouillon or salt.
2. Cover tightly and cook over low heat until tender, or water is absorbed.
3. Add butter to hot rice. Mix well.
4. Can add sauteed almonds, celery, onions, mushrooms or any combination.

Yield: 3 cups

WILD RICE PATTIES

WHAT'S NEEDED:

1 cup wild rice
1 quart salted water
2 strips bacon
1 (2 ounce) can mushrooms (stems and pieces)
1/2 clove garlic, diced to pulp
1/4 medium onion, diced fine
1/2 rib celery, diced fine
salt and pepper
2 whole eggs
2 Tablespoons butter

HERE'S HOW:

1. Cook rice in 1 quart of salted water, boiling until rice is tender and fluffy, about 30 minutes.
2. In a separate frying pan, fry bacon until crisp. Remove bacon and saute mushrooms, garlic, onions and celery until golden brown. Add to wild rice with crumbled bacon.
3. Season to taste with salt and pepper.
4. Add 2 eggs, mix thoroughly. Form into patties and fry in butter.

Note:

These may be served with 2 quail on each patty with Brandied Peach Sauce (see index). Wild rice patties may also be served separate with orange marmalade.

STUFFED POTATO

WHAT'S NEEDED:

6 large, cold baked potatoes
1/2 cup sour cream (chive and onion type)
1/4 cup grated Cheddar cheese
salt and pepper
paprika

HERE'S HOW:

1. Cut baked potatoes in half lengthwise, scooping out the potato. Save shell.
2. Grate potato with a grater or food processor.
3. Mix grated potato, sour cream and cheese together thoroughly.
4. Season to taste with salt and pepper.
5. Stuff potato shells with this mixture.
6. Sprinkle paprika on top.
7. Bake at 375 degrees for about 35 minutes or until they are golden brown.

12 Servings

FINISHING FACTS

CARE

Care in the field is vital to the quality of any meat. The animal, bird or fish, should be dressed immediately after killing and skinned as soon as possible. The greatest degree of sanitation in field preparation should be used. Cleanliness is of the greatest importance.

COOKING

The wild animal or bird is inclined to have less natural fat, therefore may have a tendency for dryness. Dryness can be overcome by placing a slice of beef suet on top of the meat and cooking slowly, or by larding. Larding is accomplished by threading a needle with thin strips of beef suet and pulling the suet strip through the meat at 2 inch intervals.

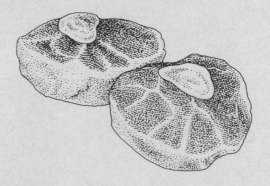

SMOKED GAME

Nearly all wild game, fish, fowl or red meat is receptive to a liberal libation of hickory smoke. We have made no attempt in this book to explain the fine art of smoking meat. There are many capable locker plant operators and other commercial smokers available. I suppose that the ''do it yourself'' route could prove to be most interesting. If you have a yen to do it yourself in small quantities, there are many good books available. I have always found the larger fish, 15 pounds and up to be excellent when smoked. Smoked wild boar is a classic. (Served with a cold Cumberland or Horseradish Sauce, it is a feast fit for a King.) Smoked duck, pheasant, goose and turkey are delicacies that will do marvelous things for an hors d'oeuvre table.

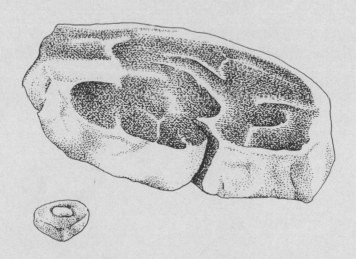

CANNING OF BIG GAME

Chill meat 36 to 48 hours after killing. Soak in salt water (1/4 cup salt to 1 quart water) 1 to 2 hours. Wipe meat, cut with lengthwise grain, removing fat, gristle and bones.

COLD PACK:

Pack raw meat: add 1/2 teaspoon salt per pint, but no liquid. Set open sterilized jars in large pan with warm water 2 inches below rim of jars. Cover pan. Simmer until medium done about 75 minutes. Adjust lids; process in pressure canner 75 minutes for pints and 90 minutes for quarts at 10 pounds pressure.

HOT PACK:

Cook meat from 1/3 to 1/2 done by roasting, broiling, braising or frying. Pack hot meat loosely, 1 inch from top jar; add 3 to 4 Tablespoons broth or cooking fat for each jar. Add 1/2 teaspoon salt per pint. Process at 10 pounds pressure in canner for 90 minutes for quarts and 75 minutes for pints.

CANNING OF UPLAND GAME

COLD PACK:

Pack raw meat into sterilized jars to within one inch of top. Leave the bones in, add no liquid, add 1/2 teaspoon salt per pint, seal, process in pressure canner at 10 pounds pressure for 80 minutes-boned or 75 minutes with bone in.

HOT PACK:

Simmer until medium done. Remove bone or pack with bones in, leaving pieces for frying. Pack hot in sterilized jars, add 1/2 teaspoon salt per pint, cover with hot broth, process in pressure canner at 10 pounds pressure for 75 minutes-boned, for 90 minutes with bone in for quart size jars. Pint jar — 65 minutes-boned, and 75 minutes with bone in.

Giblets — Precook in broth or water until medium done. Add 1/2 teaspoon salt per pint. Pack hot, cover with hot broth and process in pint jars, 10 pounds pressure for 75 minutes.

INDEX

NOTES

NOTES

NOTES

AS SERVED IN COLLINS BACKROOM

*An International
Buffet Table of Wild Game*

North American Bison

Australian Rabbit

New Zealand Venison

Sauce Bordelaise

Chinese Ringneck Pheasant

French Rouen Duckling

Brandy Peach Sauce

Rack of Canadian Black Bear

Served with Appropriate Appetizers

hors d'ouevres, side dishes and wines